PRAISE

This book is a masterclass in how to succeed in business and in life. Many of us have our share of rebuilding to do after these last couple of years, and 6-Figure Blueprints will help you to assemble the kind of business you want, and to do it your way.
Shawn Johal | Business Growth Coach, Elevation Leaders, Bestselling Author of The Happy Leader

6-Figure Blueprints is itself a blueprint for navigating these turbulent financial times. These entrepreneurs' stories offer a way forward as we rebuild in the wake of the COVID-19 pandemic.
Orad Elkayam | Founder, Mogi Group

There is much wisdom gained from the insights of others experiences when shared in a manner that seeks to leave a mark in a beneficial way. Entrepreneurship, leadership, non-profit growth, corporate attainment or whatever your goals are in life, sometimes the best learning comes from reading the successes and hardships of others. This is a read I recommend to anyone who wants to understand the real, gritty, but rewarding work of entrepreneurialism. 6-Figure Blueprints is a refreshing peek behind the curtain of what makes businesses thrive.
Paul L. Gunn Jr | Founder & CEO, KUOG Corporation

How do you encourage entrepreneurship? I think it's a few simple reminders: Put in the work, find your passion, and stay crazy. When you feel out of place or like you're not doing anything, just remember that it's your responsibility to find out who you are and what you want. The best way to be an entrepreneur is to never stop being an entrepreneur. 6 Figure Blueprints and Beyond is the pick-me-up read that gives those looking to make a leap into entrepreneurship that "Chicken Soup" boost to take that first step.

Aaron Vick | Muti-X Founder, Web3 Futurist, Technology Evangelist, Author of Inevitable Revolutions: Secrets and Strategies for a Successful Business and more

This book is overflowing with wisdom from successful entrepreneurs all over the world. Whether you're looking for inspiration or motivation, there's something in these stories for you.

Glenn Hopper | CFO, Sandline Discovery and Bestselling Author of Deep Finance

This anthology curates essays from successful entrepreneurs who detail the highs and lows of their experience in the world of business. To be the best, you have to learn from the best, and this book connects you directly to the source.

Tamara Nall | CEO & Founder, The Leading Niche

We're living in unprecedented times, that's undeniable, but the wisdom and insight gained by those who came before us can guide us toward a prosperous tomorrow. You'll find no shortage of that wisdom and insight in 6-Figure Blueprints.

Rick Yvanovich | CEO, TRG

All of the greatest entrepreneurs have one thing in common: they listen to and learn from the best. In Six-Figure Blueprints, entrepreneurs from all industries and walks of life share their tried-and-true advice to help you draw up the blueprint for your dream business.

Sabrina von Nessen | Speaker, Mentor & Author | Expert for Emotional Leadership

Business leaders all over the world have found themselves back to the drawing board in recent years. Whether you're faced with a total blueprint redraw or just looking for a little inspiration to power through this pandemic, you'll find plenty of food for thought in this anthology.

Rodney Stamps | USA Today & WSJ Bestselling Author | Co-Author of 90 Days to Live: Beating Cancer When Modern Medicine Offers No Hope | Co-Author of Quitless: The Power of Persistence in Business and Life | Co-Founder at Attacking Cancer, LLC

It doesn't get any more real than the stories in Six-Figure Blueprints. Do yourself a favor and enrich yourself through the example set by these entrepreneurs at the height of their careers and watch your business begin to build itself.

Levantay Vanessa OConnor | CEO, Levantay Enterprise LLC & USA Today Bestselling Author

6-FIGURE
BLUEPRINTS
AND BEYOND

HOW 50 ENTREPRENEURS MADE
IT AND HOW YOU CAN TOO

ALINKA RUTKOWSKA

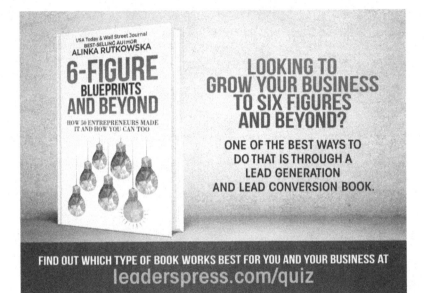

TABLE OF CONTENTS

INTRODUCTION

"**W**hat's the plan?"

When you start a business, this question might be thrilling to hear. You have the opportunity to share your dreams, visions, and next steps in your answer. The future looks bright, and the floor plan that you have envisioned for the world is one step closer to becoming a reality.

. . .until that plan needs to be tossed in the wastebin, wiped down completely, or put in a drawer for a later date.

The COVID-19 pandemic stalled many plans that many entrepreneurs had for the next year, two years, or five years. Projects came to a grinding halt. Businesses shut down completely. The world seemed to stop for months on end.

But as you'll learn, not all entrepreneurs took this pandemic as a time to close up shop. Some simply took an eraser to their blueprints and started to redraw the vision that they had for their business, their community, or their world. Others continued to build on what they already had, adjusting and adapting to the "new normal."

When asked, "What's the plan?" again after six months, a year, or five years, the answer may be very different. But the beautiful thing about blueprints, we have learned in the past two years, is that they are simply plans—they are not permanent. And if you rework them enough, that blueprint will help you build a six-figure business.

Six-Figure Blueprints is the fifth installment in the *Supreme Leadership* anthology series. You'll read stories from 34 business leaders who made plans, took an eraser to their plans, expanded plans from other leaders, and worked meticulously to make their plans a reality for decades. You'll read about leaders who had to completely change direction during the COVID-19 pandemic and those who started businesses *because* of the COVID-19 pandemic.

These leaders run very different businesses (from an event space in New York City to a dessert shop in South Carolina to a private healthcare business in Edmonton) but they've explored many of the same challenges while drawing up a six-figure blueprint:

- Perfecting their product or service
- Following their passion vs. Following the money
- Building a team to see their plans through
- Measuring, taking, and assessing risks

When you consider all of these challenges and the outside factors that are out of our control, it's no wonder that our authors advise to *keep an eraser nearby* or *never give up.*

Even though the global pandemic affected many businesses in a negative way, there is something to be said for the innovation, creativity, and adaptability that helped many of our authors change, scrap, or create entirely new six-figure blueprints. The stories, lessons, and wisdom in this anthology might not have been shared if it weren't for the COVID-19 pandemic. No one had this era in their blueprint, but that's exactly why the "drawing board" is stacked with erasers, wipes, and new sheets of paper.

PUTTING PEN TO PAPER

Baking and Business
Ben Hall, CEO of Big Ben's
Desserts and Ice Cream

E ntrepreneurship is something you can create within yourself. I believe that you can take an average person, teach them the skills they need to build a six-figure business, and turn them into a successful entrepreneur. But I also believe that some people are born with a very unique spirit; because of who they are and the qualities that they have, they gravitate toward entrepreneurship. Before I started Big Ben's Desserts and Ice Cream, I knew I had that spirit and I felt confident about starting my own business, but I certainly didn't know that I'd be laying out the blueprints for a cake shop.

When you're looking to dive into entrepreneurship, you can use many different blueprints to help guide you. Entrepreneurs can replicate, copy, or tweak the plans that were laid out before them. But I don't work like that. When I looked into starting my own business, I looked to myself. What did I have to bring to the table? What skill sets did I have?

Self-fulfillment, to me, is success. I think you've reached success when you can personally be fulfilled about what you're doing day in and day out. I believe that money doesn't necessarily measure success, although we live in a society where we focus on six, seven, or eight figures as a sign of success. Because I was able to fulfill myself first, reaching that six-figure milestone was just another part of my journey. To be successful in business, you have to be fulfilled by it in some shape, form, or fashion. It's the only way you can wake up every day and attack the problems that come with running a business. Before you start laying out your blueprints, you have to determine what will fulfill you and what makes up your definition of success.

The Banana Pudding That Started It All

In 2009, I was doing a lot of reading, praying, and meditating. I was looking for the skills and passions that would be the center of my next business. And then I made a banana pudding.

I made a banana pudding for me. I didn't make it for anybody else and I didn't have plans on selling it, much less opening up a dessert business. But that banana pudding was really good. I made a another one and brought it to a Thanksgiving party for work; everybody fell in love with it. They asked me if I baked cakes, and I said no. But I started thinking that maybe this banana pudding was something of value that I could bring to the marketplace.

Baking is a very precious gift. When you bake something for somebody, you're automatically competing with their grandma, their aunt, or whoever made their favorite pie from childhood. If I wanted to make a business out of making banana pudding and baking cakes, I had to make the *best* cakes that people had ever eaten. When it comes to baking, I believe in quality over quantity.

Step by step, I started making the transition and teaching myself how to bake. Baking is a science, and there's not much room for error. You can't leave out ingredients. You can't play around with banana pudding. You get one time to make your batch right and bake it how it's supposed to be baked. If you're even thinking about starting a baking business, your main focus has to be on the product.

I started giving my cakes away just to build confidence and get feedback. I did this for two years straight until I heard enough people say that my cakes were the best they ever had. And in the meantime, I was learning about how I could build a business off of giving people sweet attacks from my banana pudding.

I knew that revenue and six figures would come if I got my recipes right. Money wasn't my first concern. When you're starting a business, you have to focus inward first. You're the head of your business—you have to improve yourself before you can improve your business. Everything that you do, from the prices you set your cake at to the feeling a customer has when they leave your space, is a reflection of you as the owner. Revenue can certainly be a form of success, but that success is only going to come from your ability to fulfill your personal goals.

Through my business, I've been fortunate to be able to touch a lot of lives. Big Ben's isn't just about a slice of cake or banana pudding. My business is built on making an impact in the community. Money just happened to come with the vision. It's also needed to support the vision. Our community has come together in a beautiful way to support the business because the business is supporting the community. Everybody who comes into our shop is made to feel like somebody—we want to touch your life and impact your day in some form. I knew that if I was able to do that first and foremost, the money would come later.

Not only do entrepreneurs have to focus inward, but you also have to perfect your craft to reach the six-figure milestone. I could have opened a shop with the first cake that I made. I could have launched a big marketing campaign, pushed the product on social media, and partnered with people who would bring the community into the shop. But my cake wouldn't have been perfect, and people wouldn't have come back. People are always going to want the best of the best. They're going to go out of their way to afford the best that money can buy—and they're going to come *back* for the best that money can buy with a bunch of friends. Word of mouth, to me, is one of the strongest forms of advertisement. But it's only going to work if you perfect your craft.

Perfecting your craft is also going to fulfill you as you build the business and grow your customer base. Pour all of your time, energy, and focus into actually perfecting whatever product or service that you want to provide first. When you do that, everything else will fall into place.

Assess and Evaluate Your Recipe

This process doesn't end when you open your doors or hit six figures. Every time you want to take your business to the next level, you will have to go through a period of self-assessment and self-evaluation. Keep perfecting your craft, and keep looking for what is going to fulfill you.

From time to time, you'll have to look at your business from a bird's eye view. Go back to the drawing board, start from scratch, and look at where you can enhance your business. How can you do more than what you did yesterday? Taking things to the next level requires looking at the simple things: where you can cut costs, which position to hire, etc. Maybe you need more space to hold more products, or you just need to refresh your team on the customer service standards that you built your business on at the beginning. Just like in baking, changes don't have to be huge to make a huge difference.

As Big Ben's has grown, I've remained very hands-on and used my self-assessment and self-evaluation to make changes. Baking isn't something you can just give over to someone else. Your team has the same care and mindset as you—and I think that more business owners need to hold that same mindset, even if they're not selling cakes.

I think a lot of businesses fail when they pass their production off too soon. We all want to grow our businesses, but when you grow too fast, you're going to risk building a team that doesn't have the love and care that you have for your business. Love is definitely the most important ingredient that you need to bake, whether you're just making a cake for your grandkids or you're running a commercial business. It's also a key ingredient for running a business. Everything has to be done with love and care.

I say, never leave your home without your hand towel, broom, and your dustpan. Even when your business reaches six and seven figures, you have to always be prepared to step in and fill any role that's needed to protect the integrity and service of the business. A lot of owners get out of the picture too soon. They think that once they hit six figures, they never have to be around to close up shop or clean up around the office. If you're willing to stick around, you're going to build a stronger foundation to where, when you finally do step away, you can go travel out the country and still be able to make money. Your team will do a better job when they see you showing up to work and doing the best job *you* can. For a while, that means picking up the hand towel and working side by side with everyone on your team.

There's Always a New Recipe to Make

This humility circles back to the moments when you first decide to open a business. You have to see your business as a reflection of you. You have to align your goals with your self-fulfillment and not just dollar signs. Building a business is an investment, but it also requires an investment in yourself.

Sitting down with this anthology is an investment in yourself, so you're on the right track. I am committed to reading books, listening to podcasts, and learning something new every day. Life is unpredictable. Running a business is unpredictable. There will always be a reason to quit or give up. You can prepare for that by investing in yourself and building a strong mindset to overcome the many obstacles that will continue to come at you every single day.

You have to keep yourself in shape, mentally. Building a six-figure business is a marathon, not a sprint. When one challenge is conquered, another one will rise up. Even when you spend years perfecting your craft, there will always be a critique of it. Someone will have something nasty to say. You can't let these things break you; you have to have a strong mindset. The best way to develop a strong mindset is to know that every day, you are putting in the work and doing your best to reach the self-fulfillment that you seek for yourself. That self-fulfillment isn't always going to mean dollar signs or seven figures. Look within yourself. Find a product, service, or a craft that you want to perfect. And then continue to perfect this as you build out certain processes, open a business, and expand. There is always a new recipe to make or a new ingredient to experiment with. Whether you try something new, learn from it, and improve is up to you.

My Passion for Bargains
Jody Steinhauer,
Founder and President of
The Bargains Group

Twenty years ago, I won every award you can imagine for The Bargains Group. To some people, this looks like success. But business leaders kept coming up to me and asking,

"Why do you care about the homeless?"

"Why do you spend so much time helping these people?"

"Are you a businessperson or what?"

I always reminded them that it's not the amount of money that's in the bank that matters. Six figures, seven figures, eight figures—it doesn't make me successful. Success is being able to live out what I want people to talk about in my eulogy. I draw my blueprints so that every day, I can be the best that I can be. Every day, I want to walk away and write down three awesome things that I've done. The most awesome thing, to me, is helping people with whatever they need. I love helping people; I love knowing that I've impacted someone's life in a positive way. Yes, this passion helps direct my business decisions, but it also carries over into my personal life.

There were so many opportunities to help people during the COVID pandemic. I continued paying my child's tutor the same rate, even though we did virtual tutoring, and brought them more jobs from some of my friends. Before COVID really hit the fan, The Bargains Group was able to buy up everything you can possibly find on the marketplace and send those supplies to homeless shelters, correctional facilities, nursing homes, long-term care, and first responders across the great nation of Canada. Just last night, I sat and listened to my children while they had a nervous breakdown over having a math test. The opportunities to help people do not end when business open back up or situations get less dire.

It doesn't matter *what* I'm doing—I just want to help people. That authentic desire, combined with a consistent moral compass, were the pencil and ruler that helped me draw out the six-figure blueprint for The Bargains Group, Promotional Products Company, and Kits for a Cause.

What is The Bargains Group?

Entrepreneurship and bargains have always been in my blood. Since I got out of school many years ago, I've only worked for two or three other people. In all three of those jobs, I was the best employee my boss had ever had. I was able to help people. I have always run my part of the company like it was *my* company.

Part of this was being frugal. I always looked for a bargain, using resilience and grit along the way. When I was on the road, I would take all of the pens and notepads from the hotels I stayed in, and I would tell my boss to slash our office supply budget.

I didn't set *out* to be an entrepreneur, but the opportunity came along, and I took it, 32 years ago. At the time, I was in my early twenties: single, no kids, and running the wholesale division of another company like it was my company. But outside of my office, things weren't looking good. The company had decided to declare bankruptcy due to a poor business decision. I was making the company millions of dollars, but they were having serious financial issues.

On a Friday during this time, my boss walked into my office and said that he would set me up with a new job, in a new office, without any support staff. He offered me 10 percent of the profits and part ownership of this new company. When I went home and thought about the offer, I realized that I *was* the company. I was already running things. What did I have to lose in going off on my own, with no support team, and being the only owner of a new company?

I already had the name "The Bargains Group" registered; I had been doing deals on the side, but never dove into the deep end of entrepreneurship. The risk was worth it. I planned to open up shop Monday morning, and because I had already established my passion for bargains, all of the factories and the suppliers all over Canada got wind of my big move over the weekend. They all called me, telling me they'd supply my products, whatever I needed, and I could pay them when I got paid.

As a twenty-something taking her first steps as an entrepreneur, I thought that was a pretty nice way to open a business. But I wasn't surprised by my quick success. All the suppliers already grew to trust me throughout my career. They sent me hundreds of thousands of dollars with the product because my reputation was already golden. They knew that I would never order product if I couldn't pay for it. I didn't need to draw a blueprint aiming for six figures because I knew The Bargains Group was going to be a hundred-thousand-dollar business from day one. I knew it would be that successful because I knew the kind of dollars and figures that I was doing for other people, when I didn't even own the company.

Back when I started The Bargains Group, Canada hadn't caught up to the bargain shopping trend. I used to go across the border all the time to Detroit and go on crazy bargain shopping trips at places like Kmart and TJ Maxx. When I started my company, there were very few discount wholesalers of clothing and basic items. I pioneered that sector, but not because I saw this potential to make six figures overnight—it was all because I wanted to help people.

With the success of The Bargains Group, I was able to start another company, Promotional Products Company. That fared well, and I could focus more on my passion, which is ending homelessness. I had already spent a lot of time volunteering at homeless shelters and found there was a massive need for the discount items that I provided to them. In 2013, we started Kits for a Cause, a charity where we get executives together to do team-building and build kits to donate to shelters across the country.

Today, The Bargains Group is still kicking. I have a thirty-two-year-old company with no salespeople. Nobody's doing business development for us—that says something about all of our success. In 2021 alone, we've helped 1,800 brand-new clients this year, just on referral, and people finding us and hearing about us through word of mouth. It's been a horrible year for many, and our company has almost doubled.

All of this success would mean nothing if The Bargains Group couldn't help people. My numbers are larger than when I originally worked in retail, but I still get just as excited by helping people get a bargain. Whether I sell underwear to a retail store and teach them how to merchandise it and how to offer a client two-for-one, or it's a local homeless shelter that desperately needs underwear for the women, I get excited by connecting the dots and helping people. No matter how much money they're giving me in return, I am always committed to making their eyebrows raise and wowing them.

Follow Your Passion

We have been in business for 32 years, and we're just getting started. I'm ready for another 32 years of The Bargain Group! Unless you love what you do, and you're ready to do it 24/7 for the next 50 years, I wouldn't recommend being an entrepreneur. If the idea of running your business and solving problems for the next 50 years excites you, do it! If you do love what you do that much, the buckets of money will start pouring in, but don't worry about that. Worry about being the best at what you are passionate about; worry about how you can continue to learn, grow, and be better. When you worry about that, the money will look after itself.

This should be your philosophy when you start a business or decide to grow your business. What is it that you're passionate about? What do you love doing? If it's nothing, you've got to hire someone to do everything for you, so you have time to go out and explore what you really love. The moment I realize that I don't love being an entrepreneur, I know I will hire someone to run all of my companies for me so I can focus on more charitable work and following that passion.

Following my passion, whether that means stepping aside from my business or even starting another one, is always what I've done.

My passion for bargains and my passion for helping people has always led the way. It's led to six, seven, eight figures—but only because I love every step of the way.

Do not be afraid to follow your passion, even if that means taking a surprising path. My parents were not happy when I told them I was going into fashion. I got a 98 percent average in school—everyone expected me to be a doctor or a lawyer. But I didn't let their disappointment keep me from following my passion. I would tell them that they should be proud I was going into fashion because I was going to be successful in fashion. I was going to be successful in anything that I loved doing, and I would always make more money than the doctors and lawyers in my family. If I had decided to be a doctor or a lawyer, following the money rather than my passion, I probably would have made a lot less than I'm making now!

From day one, I've always followed this moral compass to lead me to what I wanted to do. My passion always pointed me in the direction that I wanted to go. And because I was so confident in where I was going, I knew I would be able to identify and navigate any roadblocks in my way. I was so confident that I knew I'd bring people along with me on my journey.

If you want to be an entrepreneur and draw up a six-figure blueprint, you have to find what makes you this confident and this passionate. You may let people down *until* the money starts rolling in. That's okay. If we follow what we love to do, no clock will watch us. If we follow what we love to do, the money and the time and the effort that we put into it will be natural.

Riding the Wave
Jeroen Kraaijenbrink,
Founder of Do Strategy

As someone who has built a business as a strategy consultant, I should probably have a detailed explanation of the blueprint I drew that got me where I am today. I don't. The journey that got me to where I am today feels more like a surfing trip than building by a strict blueprint. If you've never been out surfing, it goes like this. Every time there's a wave, you can look at where that wave will take you based on the choices you make. If the surf is good, you can see another wave or two a bit further toward the horizon. You have the ability to pick which wave you want to ride until you reach the shore, and then you do it all again when you paddle back onto the water.

The story of my six-figure business is something closer to that than a detailed blueprint. I never had the intention to get my PhD until I saw that "wave" coming as I was finishing my final project for graduation. I never saw myself as an entrepreneur until the saw the "wave" of need for my specific skills and specialty. Throughout my career, my focus has been more on what moves were possible rather than holding onto a larger goal or mission statement that was meant to encourage my every move. I don't really believe in high-level mission or vision statements—they are more likely to emerge while you move forward than successfully dictate how (or if) you move forward. As long as I feel better with each next step, I'm not worried about where I'm going two, three, or four next steps from now. I'll get to the next wave when I paddle back into the ocean.

This approach has helped me build a six-figure business and maintain my role as a professor. I also run a business helping companies develop their new strategy for the coming year and implement it. In addition to those projects, I'm also training at two Executive MBA programs, where I help, usually mid-level managers, learn how to do strategy.

The business ventures were a natural addition to my career in academia. After earning my PhD, I became an assistant professor and then an associate professor. I enjoyed working with students, but I preferred working with people who already had a business. I also wanted to have a more direct impact on practicing businesses. So instead of working full-time in academia, I chose to ride the entrepreneurial wave and spend part of my time in academia and part of my time as a consultant and trainer. Riding this wave didn't happen overnight; gradually, step by step, I got my first clients and held first lecture in an MBA program. From there on, it expanded every year.

What Are You Good At?

Everything that I do has grown out of my specialty in strategy. If you are looking to ride the next wave of your life, you have to first discover what you are good at and what makes you unique compared to your peers. Search internally. What are you good at? What do you like to do? What industries do you want to explore? What can you do that no one else can? Be authentic and look at what you can bring to the table with your perspective. Discovering this answer will help you immensely as you build your strategy *and* separate yourself from everyone else in your industry.

Time and again, through working with entrepreneurs, I've seen that looking at the market is not the way forward. Don't look at what the market needs—if you try to force talents and interests, you won't last long in the industry you choose.

Once you have a hold of the niche you want to explore, I think it's important to try a bunch of different things. I still do a little bit of research. I do student supervision at the university. I teach, I have a couple of books, I write for Forbes, and I do consulting. Not all of these projects or titles have helped me reach six figures in my business, but they have all allowed me to explore different avenues related to strategy. You have to be willing to try new things, even though you're not going to succeed at all of them. If you're riding a wave that's taking you nowhere, you can move yourself away from it and better spend your time riding a better wave. That's what my journey has been all about, and it all started with looking internally at where I excel.

Looking in will not only reveal the positive traits and interests that you have, but also limiting beliefs that have been holding you back from even *looking* to the next wave. If you want to build a six-figure business, you have to overcome these limiting beliefs.

Of course, that's easier said than done. But start by making the switch from thinking, "Why me? Why could I do this? Why should I be able to make six figures or seven figures?" to "Why not me?" This switch was pivotal in me taking the first steps to starting my own business. Why should I be making less than anyone else who has the education and experience that I have in strategy? Why shouldn't I be charging prices that I know my clients are willing to pay?

Of course, my mindset hasn't shifted so far toward me thinking that I'm perfect and that I'm going to see six-figure success at everything I do. I know I'm going to make mistakes, and I'm ready to make mistakes. Every entrepreneur and every person are going to make mistakes when they try something new. Limiting beliefs holds you back from trying something new in the first place—so overcome those beliefs, pursue what you are good at, and be ready to make mistakes along the way.

Mistakes Aren't Wasted Time

Before COVID, I started building the blueprints to develop a self-paced, e-learning environment. The pandemic only accelerated this project froward; I invested loads of time into it for two years. But I've recently come to realize that this isn't the wave that I want to be riding. I have books and articles that I can give to students who want to learn from me at their own pace. If students *want* to engage with me, I don't want to do so online. I like to be engaged with my students in real-time, in person. I find that my strengths lie in listening and giving feedback.   Although the project is still up, it didn't take off like I had originally anticipated—and I know it's because it doesn't play to my strengths and what I bring to the table. But I don't see the past two years as a waste of time. I might have made a mistake in thinking that I would thrive creating a self-paced class online, but I didn't waste my time learning that it was a mistake. As I've come to terms with the failure of the project, I've been spending more time learning what moves will be better for me and my business in the future. Maybe I can still pivot in a way that plays to my strengths but also satisfies the needs of students who may be affected by the COVID-19 pandemic, their location, or other factors. I don't have all the answers yet, but I know that they're out there.

Not everything that you do as an entrepreneur is going to take off. What matters is that you tried something within your field of study, expertise, or industry. As long as you have a core that you are branching off of, you'll be able to come back to square one, find the next wave to ride, and get back on your feet in no time.

Success Is More than Money

I'm not too worried about the failed e-learning project because I'm succeeding in so many other areas. My business is succeeding, I'm succeeding as a professor, and I'm succeeding as a writer.

Success means more to me than just a paycheck. Money is, of course, a driver. If there's more money coming in, I'm not going to complain. Money coming in is a reminder that I am capable of building a customer base and meeting the promises that I have set for them. But I also measure my success using various metrics. Returning customers is a sign of success. When customers come back to me, I know that I didn't just tell a great story or market myself well—I actually delivered on the promises that I made. Students who thank me for my guidance is a sign of success. A high number of viewers on my blog posts is a sign of success. All of these metrics play into where I think I am in my industry; I like to have an audience and make not just a qualitative impact, but also a quantitative impact.

Ultimately, I want to make the most impact on people as I can. I want to impact a lot of people and I want them to walk away satisfied after reading my books, hearing my lectures, or sitting in a strategy meeting with me.

I'm sure I will find other ways to make this impact. I've let go of any limiting beliefs that hold me back from trying new things or exploring new avenues within my niche. What will these new things be? It depends on what waves are rolling up next.

You Need to Be Crazy
Darya Yegorina,
Founder of CleverBooks

A very powerful, rich CEO gets a visitor one day—a young man. The young man tells the CEO that he wants to marry the CEO's daughter. The CEO asks, "Why would my daughter marry a poor man like you? She deserves the president of an international bank." So, the young man goes to an international bank and says, "I'd like to become the president of this bank." A man at the bank says, "Why should you be the president? You don't have experience!" The young man claims that he is the son-in-law of the very powerful, rich CEO. The bank gives the young man the position and the very powerful, rich CEO gives the young man his blessing to marry his daughter.

You might have heard this joke before—it's all about the importance of faking it until you make it. A lot of entrepreneurs and people in Silicon Valley claim to use this strategy to rise to the top. I have to tell you—it works.

When I started CleverBooks, I didn't lie like the young man in the joke. We told the truth, but we had the confidence of the young man when we began having conversations about contracts. And with the "fake it until you make it" strategy in our minds, we secured our first contract with a customer. We secured our first speaking engagement at a conference. We "faked it" until we made it. Sound crazy? I tell *all* entrepreneurs that they have to be a little crazy, especially if they're looking at milestones like six, seven, or eight figures.

Bringing Kids to Space

CleverBooks is a company creating digital infrastructures based on emerging technologies for education. Our main aim is to influence the digital transformation in the education sector through augmented reality. We offer comprehensive digital spaces for K-12 education where students can explore, create, and collaborate in the multiuser environments, gaining an immersive and engaging learning experience.

What this means for kids it that they can take trips to space. They can assemble their own spaceships and rockets and explore different planets. Our technologies allow children to use their imagination, be innovative, ask questions, search for answer, all in a fun way that manipulates reality. Children create their own schoolyard. They can build a whole city.

Behind all of these cool experiences, CleverBooks aims to promote inclusive education and support kids to become future innovators. We support creativity and we want to help children discover their highest potential, developing the future and building skills in and out of the digital landscape. With the digital landscape becoming more and more central in today's world, I believe that we are going the extra mile to support students in all of their educational and creative endeavors.

Many years ago, I was a small girl in school who got a first glimpse of technology while reading a book. The book had a picture of a computer in it, but I never was able to access a computer in real life until I was 20 years old. Until I could use that computer to explore the world, I was dreaming about it. The technology we have developed since I was a child offer so many possibilities in the world of education. I want technology to be affordable, accessible, and available to every kid from an early age.

In 2017, I took the plunge and decided to make those possibilities a reality. When I started CleverBooks, I was already known in the world of emerging technologies and education. People have always seen me as a crazy woman who manipulates realities, who is trying to push digital transformation in education, and who is trying to persuade teachers that using technology is nothing scary. I know that when educators take a tiny step outside their comfort zone, they can deliver something absolutely amazing to their kids. Technology can help teachers inspire students, spike their creativity, and fuel their motivation to learn. If I can help in this process, I can leave the next generation with the ability to better educate their children through augmented reality, artificial intelligence, and different emerging technologies that will continue to be developed long after I am gone.

Today, CleverBooks is helping children learn in over 62 countries around the world. We have given the opportunity to see, hear, and touch knowledge through the visualization, interaction, and creativity in an augmented reality environment. And we are going to keep pushing through until I leave the footprint that I have aspired to leave on the coming generation.

Along the way, people have told me I am crazy. I advise *them* to be crazy. To anyone with a dream, I advise them to try to combine things that are absolutely not combinable; to be dreamers and follow their dreams. Of course, dreamers still need a blueprint. When you go after your dream, have a plan on how to achieve it. Have a plan to gain strategic and tactical clients, even if that means faking it before you make it. If you believe that you can change something, you have to just go and do that. You have to be crazy.

Crazy and Creative

You have to be crazy and creative *especially* if you want to hit the six- and seven-figure milestones. You need to put bold ideas on the table and see them through. At CleverBooks, we have a team of developers. I will come up with the idea and bring it to them, and often they tell me that my idea cannot be done. They tell me, "It's not going to happen." My response? "It must happen."

I believe in the six- and seven-figure potential that our products can bring to people—so even if we have to combine things that appear impossible, we have to see the idea through. The ideas that I bring to the table are not average ideas—ideas are average when they are easy to achieve and do not wow anyone. Instead, I bring *brilliant* ideas to my team.

I am always confident that my team find the way to make our ideas happen. That's it—it's as easy as that. I don't like when people come to me with a problem, and they don't have a solution ready to suggest. There are so many people that come to me with problems, and yet there are obvious solutions that can get them out of this problem. If someone hasn't thought about the solution to a problem, I don't want to hear them complain about it.

Anyone who is hoping to draw up a six-figure blueprint should be looking for solutions. There are solutions everywhere! The possibilities and opportunities to solve problems and expand your business are endless. Not only do we live in a world with rapidly developing technology, but we also live in a world of globalization. Everything is possible. Today's world has no boundaries; we are all interconnected. It doesn't matter which part of the world you're based in—you can always sell also on the other side of the world. You can always connect to the other side of the world. You can always hire from the other side of the world. With so many possibilities, how could we not find the solutions to all of the problems ahead of us?

When I encounter problems, I search for solutions. My team and I immediately brainstorm, come up with ideas, and we do not stop until we find the solution to the problems that stand between us and the ideas I have for the company. At the end of the day, when we have moved forward, my team will ask me, "How do you do that? How do you know upfront that your ideas will work, and when we tell you that it won't, you push us to think one step further?" It's because I know that with enough creativity, and enough craziness, we will get to the point where we make things work and bring all of our ideas to life.

This process is how we see out our six-figure blueprint. The technology and the advancement of the research that we do, and how we create the state-of-the-art products is what makes us a six-figure business.

Not Everyone Should Be Crazy

I am one of two founders of CleverBooks. Inna Armstrong and I are a well-balanced pair. I'm always looking to take risks; I want to push forward with the craziest ideas and the most elaborate visions. Inna doesn't hold me back, but she does give me another perspective that helps me find the right solution to the problems ahead of me. She thinks about the customers, the law, and the long-term plans that might have to change if we followed the vision I have in the moment. While I am more likely to push us outside of our comfort zones, she reminds me that these zones exist for a reason. We balance each other out, and I wouldn't be so successful in helping my team find solutions if it weren't for her.

I believe you can see your six- and seven-figure blueprints through if you have the right team, the right talents, and the right plan in place. Crazy ideas are just the start. You cannot search for the solution if you do not have a team of creative minds surrounding you. Fortunately, we have this at CleverBooks. We are a small company, but we are like a family and every member of the team is proud to be part of the CleverBooks team. And I think that's the success as well.

And what is success? For us, our first success was landing a contract with our first customer, confirming that our vision will help to solve problems in the future and is valuable to people in the education space. As we grew, our ideas of success grew to 10 customers, 100 customers, so on and so forth. Along the way, we gathered feedback to ensure that our products and our business was seeing out the vision that we longed to achieve when we opened our doors. When that feedback affirmed the path we were on, we felt successful.

Another success is the quality of the products and the research and development that we do. We have so many opportunities to work with innovative technologies. It's something that inspires our technical team every day to search for solutions, as crazy as they might sound. Every day, the team at CleverBooks is challenged to do something new, to have something interesting for the whole team, and to grow. Our team is able to support this crazy vision that I, Inna, and the leaders of CleverBooks have for the future of education and the digital transformation that will take place among our young people. And as our team continues to discover solutions, see our success grow, and see our six-figure blueprint come to life, they are reminded that what we think is crazy one day may become our reality the next.

Climbing the Ladder
Cindy Praeger,
Cofounder of Rhythm Systems

I sold one of my previous companies while I was in labor. Yes, you read that right. My team was in the middle of the transaction, and I was dictating the press release in between contractions. But that's how entrepreneurship is. You have to roll with everything that comes with this career path, no matter how funny or strange or uncomfortable the situation. You just have to roll with it.

My partner and I know this because we are serial entrepreneurs. We started our current company 14 years ago, with the goal to help middle-market CEOs to create clear growth strategies that are pertinent to their size and scaling goals. Along the way, we help them to use our software to execute them throughout the firm.

We know, both from experience and through working with our clients, how much it takes to create a six-figure business. We know what it takes to reach seven and eight figures. Working off of a six-figure blueprint requires grit, risk, and the ability to let go. Are you ready for that? Then you might just reach that six-figure mark.

Do You Have Grit?

There is a difference between having conviction in a dream and having data that's supporting that you're rising up the ladder and you'll be able to achieve that dream.

I speak to a lot of college students who want to be entrepreneurs. I want these kids, just like any business owner, to look inside themselves. Do they have grit? Are they willing to keep going when they're being told no every day, all the time, by everyone? How comfortable are they to take whatever idea they have and completely swerve when the market points them in a different direction?

Building a business is a series of risks. And you have to have grit to be able to wake up every day and risk time, effort, and the money in your savings account. If you want to build a six-figure business off of an idea, you have to be willing to ask people for money *knowing* that they're not likely to get it back. Can you have these hard conversations? Can you devote all of your time to this one idea, knowing that most startups don't last for more than a few years?

You *have* to be the person to have those conversations. You have to be the person hyping yourself up when every day, you're faced with "no" and you're forced to take yet another risk on yourself and your idea. When you're on the career path to being a doctor or a lawyer or any other type of employee, you have the path set out for you. Professors, managers, and mentors are pulling you up the mountain every step of the way. Entrepreneurship isn't like that. Part of the work is navigating your own path and showing the world how your idea can change the world. Not everyone is going to listen, but that's just one of the many risks that you have to take.

Starting a business requires risk, and it requires commitment. And to some people, that's a lot of fun. If the thrill of that risk sounds like fun, you might be suited to be an entrepreneur. If the risks sound abhorrent, you're not going to have a fun time building a business.

The Early Stages

When your business is just starting out, it's in the startup stage. At this point, you have to be open and looking at all the possibilities for where you're going to go with your business. All you have to go off of is your product, your conviction, and the total addressable market. Beyond that, there's no data that you can use to predict whether your business will hit six or seven figures.

At this stage, the least you can do is create a viable product that someone other than your family or friend is willing to buy. If you could do that at least 10 times, you've taken the first step on the ladder.

But you still won't know whether your business is going to take off because you've got to see if your customers will buy your product again. If you're offering a subscription service, like our SaaS company, you have to see whether or not your customers stay with you. Do they renew, or do they cancel? If you can't sustain customers, you're not going to get very far off the ground. You need to see the money coming in, contracts being signed, and the adoption of customers before you can even begin to think about six figures.

When we started Rhythm Systems, the metric that we wanted to hit was simply building a product and getting one customer who actually will pay. We got that. Next, we aimed for five that would pay, 10 that would pay. I remember when I hit the goal of having 10 customers who kept their subscription—we were so happy. At this point, it was only me and my partner running the company. Then, we could think about 50 subscribers. At 50, in my industry, you're real. Millions of dollars in revenue doesn't mean that you have millions of dollars in profit. You have to climb the ladder to get there before you can even think of expanding further, building a large team, and taking those big risks.

Recruiting Talent

Once you get to that stage, you've probably now risen from one or two employee-founders to five employees. Then you're moving into the five to 50 employees range, and now you're starting to add more and more customers. As you have more customers, they have more needs. As they have more needs, now you've got to recruit talent, delegate, and start letting go. That's the next step on the ladder.

You know why a lot of businesses die when they only have one to five customers? It's because they don't have a minimum viable product that people will pay for. You know why a lot of businesses die when they're much further up on the ladder? It's because they don't know how to recruit talent and let go.

When you are first starting out, your business is your baby. You are risking everything for it, every single day. But babies grow up, and you have to let them go. It's not easy. By the time you've gotten to a point where you can scale and really take things to the next level, you're about to get into a very uncomfortable position. You will no longer be the only one making all the decisions and knowing everything in your firm. You have to be ready to delegate and let go.

Doing everything for a business with one or two employees is feasible. If you try to do everything for a much larger business as one human being, you'll fail. One person running a company can't scale.

If you want to scale, you need to be prepared to recruit, or find a partner who is good at recruiting. You have to build a team and set up departments; this is where many people get stuck. Everything that was working got you at 50 customers may not work when you're trying to reach 100 and 200. You've got to find a way to do things differently to grow in much bigger numbers. You're no longer growing by one or 10—you have to grow by hundreds.

Change Your Mindset

You have to have much better and thoughtful strategy in order to make the transition from slowly growing to *really* scaling your business. That's where companies like Rhythm Systems comes in and saves the day.

Your strategy during this transition has to come from a completely different mindset. When your company was small, you were taking bets on everything, every day. And you could—you were the one person who was going to win or lose from taking those bets. You had nothing to lose. Now, you're making big bets and you have money. Every bet could be a million-dollar bet, and you cannot place your bets on everything. You have a lot more to lose. You have got to learn where you are going to place your bets and you've got to be able to be a little more patient to stay the course.

Think of your mindset as your weapon. When you play a much larger game, you have to learn how to play with different weapons and skills. Growth requires a lot of reworking your mindset, and that might mean facing a lot of inner turmoil. When I say "inner," I don't just mean inside your own heart and mind. I'm talking about within your company, too. The challenges you face working with five people are different than the challenges you face working with 500 or 5,000. Pile those challenges on top of the challenges of obtaining more customers and you've got one complicated business to run.

There's no way around it—we see it every day when we work with our clients. Life gets complicated when you're scaling. It seems easier from the outside, but it gets complicated.

Making an Impact

The journey from one customer and one employee to 100 customers and 500 employees is long, risky, and complicated. But serial entrepreneurs like me *love* this journey. Sure, a lot of people do it for the money. They equate money to success. But a lot of these people bow out when they realize how hard the journey is. For me, as an entrepreneur, I get up every day and face these challenges for something way more important than money. I've climbed these ladders and taken risks for impact. That's what drives me—the impact I can make on others.

When I sit down to reassess where I am and where I want to be, I ask myself, "How much impact am I having on the people who are working with me? How much impact am I having on the clients we are serving and the community at large?" Throughout my career, whether I was selling unique and rare flowers, establishing schools through the Bill and Melinda Gates Foundation, or growing Rhythm Systems, I've asked myself these questions. The answers have driven all of the decisions I make when I start businesses, scale them, and help other CEOs do the same.

When it comes to Rhythm Systems, seeing the impact of our CEOs and helping them to achieve their dreams and goals really drives me to keep taking risks and keep going. Every time I hear directly from a client that they made a breakthrough, I save the correspondence. I call them love notes. These love notes make my day. Because I've recruited well, my entire team is that way, too. We put impact above everything else.

Of course, I understand that we have to make profit to pay for our salaries and to do the things that we need to do. But every step that we've taken up that ladder, from taking risks every day to delegating when it was necessary to shifting our mindset through our periods of growth—we do it all for these love notes. I have a pile of them in my office, and I look at them often. I don't have a pile of our financials year to year; they're in a database somewhere. What are you going to keep near you when you start your business? Climb up the ladder for that reason, and you'll find your way to the next step.

Nothing Replaces Work
Mark Lazarchic,
CEO of Serenity Venture Group

If I had to end up as a "serial" anything, I'm glad I ended up a serial entrepreneur. I own soda shops, a wedding supply company, a fireworks business, and I do commercial real estate. The last time I checked, I was the owner of six companies. But I didn't always have a six-figure blueprint on my desk.

The first businesses I owned didn't stick—I got bored after a few years of running a turnover painting business, and I didn't enjoy the back-breaking work of running a landscaping business. For 10 years after my first entrepreneurial pursuits, I held down a sales job to pay my bills.

That all changed when my cousin got married a few years back. Her father, my uncle, paid for the whole extravagant affair, string quartet and all. My uncle was an entrepreneur—he owned several businesses, including a vineyard that supplied wine for the wedding. And as he held a bottle of his own wine in his hand, hearing about my management position, he laughed in my face. He told me, "Boy, did you ever sell out. You took the chickenshit route. You'd have a million dollars by now if you actually took a chance out there, but you chose chickenshit, and you settled."

That moment was what I needed to pull the trigger and really think about starting a business that would stick. I was ready to follow the blueprint, even if that meant taking the biggest gamble of my life.

If you don't want to follow the chickenshit route, you can follow this blueprint and have the six figures that people know that you could make running your own business. If you *want* to take your business idea to the next level, you are going to have to build a blueprint around one four-letter word.

No, not that one.

Work.

Building a six-figure blueprint is all about work. First, you have to work—nothing replaces work. Then as you work, you have to find out *what* works. And finally, you have to hire people who are going to put in the work. And that might sound simple; but if it was, everyone would be doing it. I'm doing it, but only after I tried, failed, and finally decided that I would do anything it took to make it work.

Nothing Replaces Work

Most people have a business idea. And you know what? Any business idea has the potential to become a six-figure business if you work hard enough and repeat your processes enough. But most people don't want to take that route. They mistake a blueprint for a loan from the bank. I've seen many business owners dump $50,000 or $200,000 into a business idea with great potential, and then they just wait around for money to come rolling in. If it doesn't come rolling in, the business owner is screwed.

I learned from those mistakes before I opened Renaissance Fireworks, which is now the largest fireworks company in the state of Minnesota. Three years after my uncle told me I was taking the chickenshit route in life, I started my fireworks company. I was still working full-time. On my lunch breaks, I would go out, change my clothes, and go to meetings. The only meetings I scheduled were during 12-1. I ordered checks with numbers starting at 14,000 so vendors would think I had been in business for a long time (I hadn't). I told people to mail invoices to a certain address because I had an assistant that took care of my expenses for me (I didn't). Every expense was paid with net-30 because that's how my business operated (I had read up on net-30 minutes before I first established that policy with a supplier).

That first year of running the business, I thought my whole life was going to change. I was practicing the speech I was going to tell my jerk of a boss when I walked out of my sales job. My business partner and I were going to use what we made and invest in expanding over the next year. Everything was going to fall into place—until I calculated what we made after our first year. When all was said and done, we made $147.

My business partner decided that he wasn't going to spend another year working to barely make three figures. I didn't quit my job, take a vacation, or roll around in a pile of money. But I wasn't discouraged. I was ready to work. After 15 years in sales, I was ready to show people that I could make it. I was stubborn. And after a back injury that left me incapable of working a 9-5 schedule, I had to keep going. In those first few years of building my fireworks business, I supplemented my income by playing professional poker. I didn't stop working just because I didn't get the results that I wanted—I worked harder.

People think that you can commit 20 hours a week to a business to get it off the ground. You can't. If you're not working hard enough to make money through your business, you don't have a business. You have a hobby. Nothing can replace work, and with the 168 hours you have each week, you can dedicate 80 hours a week working with time left over. We're all guilty of fighting with idiots on Facebook or watching TV. (At least, I am). But you can't do that for 40 hours a week and expect to succeed in business. You have to spend that time working. Nothing replaces work.

Find Out What's Working

I wasn't about to give up on the fireworks company, so I had to find out what went wrong that first year. More importantly, I had to figure out what went right. Two out of the eight locations that we had opened that first year were successful, but the other six were duds. I knew that if I just focused on what had worked, I was going to start making actual money in the next few years. My business partner didn't believe me, which is why he left. But I ended up being right.

The right business plan will reach six figures if you multiply it enough. You have to find out what works and just lather, rinse, repeat. Anything can be replicated—and when that anything is making you money, you can keep repeating and repeating, at more and more locations, until you reach that six-figure goal.

Don't think that this is an easy step. I didn't discover what was working immediately, especially when most of my locations from that first year were major flops. Finding what works for your business will *take* work, and you'll still need to commit to those 50-, 60-, 70-hour workweeks. You'll have to commit to making supplemental income until you *know* what works and you can dump your money into that strategy. But entrepreneurs will find that the motivation to keep persisting comes from within. We're psychopaths that end up with multiple businesses, emailing people at 2:30 in the morning, and obsessing over what's working have a natural drive to keep going. We're never happy, so we just keep going and keep going until we find what works.

It's hard to gauge an entrepreneur's mind because it doesn't work like everyone else's. Everyone else worries about holding down a job or seeing money drop into their bank account tomorrow. We end up seeing things and thinking to ourselves, "They're not doing that right. I could do that better." With the right amount of work, an entrepreneur will discover what's working because that's our natural instinct.

Hire People Who Are Going to Put In the Work

As an entrepreneur, you can find out what works for yourself, make a living, and live just shy of that six-figure lifestyle. But taking your business from a five- to a six-figure business is the hardest step. Finding out what works and gaining a little bit of success as a business owner is already defying the odds, don't get me wrong; but if you truly want to take things to the next level, you have to hire people to work for you.

When you start bringing on new people, you need to take the giant basket of everything you handle and give it to them. That's 80 hours of work that you have to divide among a small group of people who are never going to work as hard as you. (And why would they? It's your business, not theirs').

In many ways, bringing on a team requires you to step into a cycle of finding out what is working and hiring new people. You have to know people, know how to talk to them, and know how to figure out what they are good at doing. I have an eclectic group under me, and no one can do everything perfectly. You're going to run into that when you run a business. No matter how hard you try to train someone, they'll always have weaknesses and strengths. You have to learn how to put together a group that can each excel at a handful of tasks that you need to get done you let the entire team complement each other.

Once you've built that team, you need to let them do their damn job. You're going to have a set idea on how to do things—but you have strengths and weaknesses, too. You can't micromanage your team and force them to approach everything in the same way you'd approach it. I don't care what my team does to get to the end result—I just care that they get there when I want them to get there.

Entrepreneurs are risk takers. We're gamblers and we like adrenaline. When we get to the point where we have to hire people, we're tempted to stick to the mindset that helped us launch our business off the ground. You can't do that once your business is up and running. Once you have people working for you, an established income, and revenue coming in, you can't take those big, swinging chances anymore. You have to take smaller, calculated chances.

I know this is hard. As entrepreneurs, we start something with a small amount of money and work hard to let it grow from there. Then, we have to hand over power and control of our baby. But you can't put everything out on red 22 on a roulette wheel and expect to win big every time. Your business has gotten to the point where you can't afford to lose it all on one decision. You've got to take smaller chances and you've got to limit the amount of financial damage that you are risking. When you're starting, those big risks don't matter. You've got nothing. If you lose, it doesn't matter. But when you're at that next level, the risks you take have to consider what you have built and who is building it with you. You can't risk it all and expect your team to be on board when you lose.

You start by taking a gamble, and you grow by holding back the urge to take a gamble. That's the six-figure blueprint that has helped me avoid the chickenshit route that I was so close to following for the rest of my career. If you have the entrepreneur's mindset, if you find yourself always itching to make things better, don't take the chickenshit route. Take that gamble and build your own six-figure blueprint.

Blueprints and Bootstraps
Shelia Mac, Host of
"The Shelia Mac Show"

Putting together a blueprint requires some creativity. Trust me, I know. Currently, I'm the host of the Sheila Mac Show, a podcast and radio show on NBC's KCAA Radio that helps people rebuild, reinvent, and reboot their business and personal lives. I got that show because I had written a best-selling book, *Bootstraps and Bra Straps: The Formula to Go from Rock Bottom Back into Action in Any Situation*. But before that, I was just a woman who opened a gift shop.

Before I wrote my book, I just had a story to tell. I had an interesting youth, growing up from home to home. My parents battled many health issues, including polio. They couldn't take care of me all the time. For three and a half years, I was homeless. It took me until I emancipated at fifteen and entered the foster care system that I started to pull myself up by my bootstraps. I graduated high school early, started college early, and more importantly—I got to work. I worked in events, I worked as an assistant, and I became an entrepreneur.

Throughout my career, I had to be creative. My path was never conventional. Nothing was handed to me. I drew every line on my six-figure blueprint from scratch. And now, I have the chance to share my story and my blueprint every day through my radio show, podcast, and my book.

In essence, *Bootstraps and Bra Straps* isn't just a self-help book or inspiration to redesign your life. It's a blueprint for success, whether you want to build a six-figure business or you just want to change paths. And that blueprint is based on the BOOTS formula.

In each element of the BOOTS formula, you'll find that you need to get creative in order to move forward and reach your goals. The BOOTS formula helped me get out of the situation I was in, even before I knew it was a formula or that it was something that people needed to hear in *their* situations. No matter what situation you find yourself in, creativity will get you out; creativity and pulling yourself up by your bootstraps.

B for Being

The B in the BOOTS formula stands for "being." Being is all about who you're being and what you're doing. It doesn't matter if you're working in a big company or if you're just starting out. You can still *be* a person who is moving forward. Being is about how you show up to whatever you have to do.

I ask all of my clients to ask themselves two questions: "Who am I being in all that I'm doing, and who do I need to be to get back on track?" Keeping this mantra in mind during times of change is very important.

I opened my first gift store when I was 23 years old. The business went well—I was leasing a 5,000-square-foot business for $5,000 a month and making ends meet. But I wasn't perfect. At 23, I had a lot to learn, and I learned it the hard way. But as I learned those lessons, I never forgot the person that I wanted to be, both as a business leader and a member of my community.

My gift store was a heart-based business. It was built to do more than just sell products to people in the community; it supported people in the community. My main salespeople were ladies with retail experience at large department stores. They were talented, but they were often limited by the lack of childcare available at their jobs. Many of my employees had little babies. I had my own young children at the time, so I created a section of my store away from customers where nannies could watch over my employees' babies.

Any of my employees could come in, bring their child, and know that they were being cared for while they worked. My store didn't provide commission or fancy perks that the large department stores could afford—but we gave them the chance to work right by their babies. I also offered a flexible schedule that allowed my salespeople to go to a doctor's appointment or pick up their children from school if they needed.

These policies weren't standard at the time, but it also wasn't standard for a small mom-and-pop shop to be the best employer in town. I had to be creative in order to attract top talent and keep them working for me. But I was creative. I lead with my heart. I discovered these policies after reflecting on the person I wanted to be.

O for Orientation

The first O in the BOOTS formula is for orientation. We need to have a sense of orientation in order to take the right steps forward. We need to confidently look at our situation, however many changes we have endured, and say "This is where I am."

I certainly had to identify where I was headed when I opened my first business. I was young and without many resources at my disposal. But I knew the community where my business opened, and I knew its needs. This is what identifying your orientation is all about—even when things change at the drop of a hat.

Many years later, when COVID hit, all of our businesses changed overnight. Every business owner, parent, and *person* needed to sit down and really be honest about where they were on the map of their lives. COVID spun so many people around that suddenly, we were going in a different direction. What's important in times of crisis like this is to remember that changes provide us with a new reality. Rather than focusing on whether that new reality is better or worse than our previous one, we just had to figure out our orientation and start moving in the direction that we wanted to go.

O for Order of Operation

The next O in the BOOTS formula is for "order of operation." As you've gone through the BOOTS formula, you've established who you want to be and where you want to go. Now, it's time to think about how to get there.

For some people, in order to get to a certain place in your life, you need to get food on your table, take care of your family, or have a roof over your head before you start rebuilding other areas of your life. Each of these steps takes time and planning. When you get to this second O in the BOOTS formula, you have to sit down, build a strategic plan with the people on your team. Your team could be your family, your partner, or your employees. Either way, you have to establish those next steps in order to take them.

Sometimes, these steps will be creative. In addition to offering childcare at my gift shop, I also made a strategic plan to help me get help as I was building my business. Part of this plan was working with a government program in the late 90s established by the Job Training Partnership Act. I created a learning program and was able to hire at-risk youth. The youth were mostly young adults who were emancipating from foster care, a situation that was close to my heart.

With this plan, I hired over 200 young adults as I built my gift shop. Each and every one of them became part of our family. I was able to build a team, and they were able to earn skills that they later used in higher-paying jobs elsewhere.

My order of operations wasn't just about strategy—it harkened back to my *being,* the heart that I wanted to bring to the community. Yes, they helped me run the store and get to a place in business where I am now. But the store wasn't just a success—I was having fun and fulfilling a mission that I had set for myself when the business first opened. That's the beauty of being creative, building a strategy, and seeing it through.

T for Thinking

The *t* in the BOOTS formula is for "thinking." This is where our mindset is especially important. You have a sense of self, you have goals, and you have a strategic plan telling you which step to take next. Before you take action, it's time to get your mind right.

Your mindset is going to get us through those times where you want to give up. In these moments, Tony Robbins says, you're two millimeters to success. Everyone has hit these hard times. Maybe you experienced wanting to give up your career because of COVID. Maybe you felt everything falling apart as you balanced parenthood and entrepreneurship. Maybe you're there now, asking yourself, "Well, why does this even matter? I don't even want to try anymore." The reality is, you're just two millimeters away from real success, and your mindset is the only thing that is going to remind you that you're two millimeters away from success.

As you make your way through the BOOTS formula, you start to add more people into your circle. When it comes to mindset, *thinking* will allow you to carry your whole team *and* train your team to carry on. The right training is everything. In order to maintain the success that you obtained up to this point, you have to create leaders through training and the right thinking.

My team became my family because we all shared the same mindset. Now, I started my first business quite a few years ago. Today, employees start out with a different mindset. They don't stay at a job for ten or twenty years like they used to. If the leaders in your business are on the same page and hold onto your mindset, they will stay. The right mindset builds a team of dedicated employees, a team where you don't have to keep paying to retrain people. This one strategy saves you so much money and time.

S for Stepping Up

The last letter in the BOOTS formula, s, is for "stepping up." Every other letter in the BOOTS formula has prepared you for this step. Stepping up is about taking action. Once you have identified who you want to be, your orientation, your strategy, and your mindset, you have to act. People can read books, make to-do lists, or add events to their calendar all they want—until they actually act, nothing is going to happen.

It required action to create a childcare program for my employees. It takes action to readjust after a crisis. I had to act in order to reap the benefits from the Job Training Partnership Act. And I had to act to create a training program that turned employees into family members. As the business grew, I began to give my team the responsibility of stepping up.

This is just one example of the BOOTS formula in action. In order to apply this formula to my first business (and every business venture after that) I had to be creative. I had to keep each part in the formula in mind in order to build a six-figure blueprint. In this situation, I was able to pull up my bootstraps and create not just a business, but a positive addition to our community. And you can too, no matter what situation you are in today.

Always Learning
Dolores Pérez Islas,
Co-Founder and CEO of SILMEXICO

The biggest lesson I have learned from COVID is that we cannot control everything. For some, this was a hard lesson to learn; but I see it as an opportunity to learn even more. I believe that you have to give yourself the opportunity to learn and the opportunity to receive all the lessons of life, no matter how much of your blueprint you have already drawn. Eight years into running my own business, I still consider myself a student. I will always be a student, and I consider myself lucky to learn as I grow my business every day.

I left my family when I was fourteen years old to follow my dreams of studying overseas. Learning, traveling, and growing have always been an adrenaline rush for me. Even at such a young age, I was anxious to get out into the world, understand different ways of life, and learn what I could from many different cultures.

A lot of parents would not have allowed their child to take on such a risk. I was so young when I left home! But my mother always told me, "Don't be afraid that you're going to fail." She never wanted to be the mother who discouraged her children from taking a risk. She didn't want to shield me from the pain or the discomfort of failing. She had always acknowledged that failure *does* come with pain, but she was confident that I would learn how to pass over that pain and take the lessons that would lead me to success. As my mother, she also probably saw my stubbornness more than I ever did. I continue to be stubborn to this day—if I fail once, I assure myself that I will *not* fail again.

I knew that failure would be inevitable along my path; ironically, I have always thought less about success. Above being successful, I want to be happy. My friends tell me that I am a workaholic, but that is because work does not make them happy. I don't *need* to work in order to feed my children and live a comfortable life. I work because it brings me happiness. Waking up in the morning with a new idea or addition to my blueprint drives me to see that plan through. I am happy thinking about the problems I am solving and the lessons I am learning. If I am a workaholic, it is only because work makes me happy.

If I am successful, that is why. I believe that happiness is the foundation of success. Throughout my life, I did not know that I was made to be an entrepreneur, but I did know that I was made to challenge myself, discover, grow, and learn. I also know one thing for sure: one day, I will pass away. This is the only thing that any of us can know for sure. When I pass away, I want to be happy. I want to be happy to have done everything that I wanted to do. And as I started discovering the real estate market in Belize and later in Mexico, I knew that I wanted to solve problems, overcome challenges, and learn more while building my business. This is what makes me an entrepreneur; not the desire to make six figures.

I did not dive into entrepreneurship right away. When I started becoming interested in real estate, I watched and learned from my partners. I was so lucky to work with people who had a lot more experience than myself. The people on my team were twice my age and had worked in various industries. I loved when they had instructions to give me or advice for me. Being an entrepreneur is hard; building a six-figure business is hard. I wanted as much knowledge as possible. Mentors, team members, and other people with advice to give me could help me clear out the path before it was time to walk on my own.

My early years working in real estate were all about observing, learning, and figuring out how I could avoid making the mistakes that so many people in the real estate world make. I knew it would not last forever, but I tend to follow my intuition. I knew that when it was my moment, I would know it was time to start my entrepreneurial life.

When I decided to start my own business and to create my own dream, I was always considering and remembering the advice that I had learned along the way. I had immense help building my blueprint, but I also knew that I would be on my own without support. Before, I was living in Belize, but decided to start my business in Mexico. Nobody knew who I was. Everybody who I wanted to work with was typically older, with a lot more money and resources than I had as a young entrepreneur. Nobody was going to give me any freebies or soften the blow if I fell. I had to take fewer risks, but I continued to trust my intuition. My intuition had been shaped for many years by the knowledge and lessons I had collected along the way.

Today, I am very glad that I took that risk. Eight years later, I am still the CEO of SILMEXICO Investment Properties. We work with different companies to analyze their real estate projects and not only provide a diagnostic to our clients in terms of their whole business; but we also help them to reach their maximum potential. We see all the vulnerabilities in their projects; we touch these vulnerabilities; and we bring these vulnerabilities to a place where we can convert them into something that they can use to increase their bottom line and even exceed their potential.

What I do for clients feeds into all of my passions. I want to see all the pieces of a puzzle, put them together, and discover the bigger picture. When I get a contract with a client, I feel they are my own projects. I feel like I'm working with my own business. Every client brings me that happiness that makes me such a workaholic. I want to workday and night to be able to help them to increase their revenue, expand their business, or turn vulnerabilities into assets.

I would not be able to do this if it weren't for the advice and knowledge I had received throughout my career. If you are a new entrepreneur or you have already established yourself, seek out people better than you. Surround yourself with people who know more than you. Their advice is going to help you take your business to the next level. Look for mentors. Yes, you can learn a lot from going to school or taking a course, but you will still be faced with challenges that other people have faced before you. If you can surround yourself with people who have already overcome the challenges of being an entrepreneur, you will be able to use their blueprints and their knowledge to see your way through challenges that you face.

You also have to surround yourself with dreamers and entrepreneurs that really know the pain of being an entrepreneur. I do not mean to be dramatic, but you're going to be a better entrepreneur if you can enjoy the pain of this lifestyle. There are few easy days. Challenges threaten your business constantly. But if the adrenaline rush of this stress excites you, you are likely in the right place. Use that adrenaline to gain momentum and keep pushing through the pain.

I believe that in this life, personal and professional, every single person enjoys a different level of risk. I embrace high risks for high rewards. Whether I am leaving home at 14, moving to a new country, or starting a business, I find happiness from the adrenaline rush that comes with taking risks. So, I continue to take risks!

Every day, I will encounter new risks. No one has a magic ball that will tell you whether you're going to be successful. Risks are inevitable, and what we thought we knew about risks before is nothing compared to what we know now. The lesson of the COVID-19 pandemic, at least for me, is that there are so many things out of our control. The risks we thought we were taking before are actually much higher, because the whole world can change overnight. But that does not mean that you should hold back or be afraid. Do not be afraid of taking a risk or failing. If you want to take a risk, you just have to be very creative. You have to be very, very insistent on what you have in mind in order for you to innovate your business, prepare your business, or to make a change to your blueprint when everything changes.

If you are always learning, this will come naturally.

Never Give Up
Sabrina Fiorellino, CEO at Fero International Inc.

I knew from a very early age that I wanted to be a business owner. I was raised by a single mom, and she was a business owner. She was my hero in a lot of ways. I wanted to make her proud, get the education that she wanted me to get, and do what she did. I was always looking at her.

Anything I could do to make her proud, I did. At 16 years old, I was already working in a grocery store, and I knew there was something different about me. Even at that age, I was able to advance very quickly. I started as a cashier, went to customer service, and I kept getting elevated to new positions very quickly. This gave me the validation I needed to go further. I didn't want to just work at a business—I wanted to own one.

Ever since, I've been a serial entrepreneur. I started my first company at 18. And I've learned a few things about building a six-figure business. Never give up. You have to believe in yourself and do the work, without ever giving up. You can't reach success by just believing in yourself or just doing the work. You can't reach success thinking that it will be handed to you overnight. You need to believe in yourself to the fullest extent possible and do the work until you see those six figures coming in or achieve *any* metric of success that you set for yourself.

Fero International, Inc.

In November 2020, I sold a company I had been building for four years. I've been a serial entrepreneur my whole life: I started my first company at 18, I've worked for 10 years as a lawyer doing mergers and acquisition work on Bay Street, and I built a company building roads for the government. I sold the company for various reasons, but mainly because I had a new idea that was quickly growing, and I really believed that the blueprint I was drawing for this company needed to be my focus.

By this time, Toronto was deep into the COVID-19 pandemic. It affected everyone in my family. My mom is a double lung transplant recipient and is significantly immunosuppressed. Because of COVID, surgeries were getting canceled, and there was no room in hospital, so she couldn't go to her regular appointments. If she had been at the wrong place at the wrong time, she wouldn't have gotten her transplant, and she would have died.

My brother is an anesthetist who's intubating COVID patients; my sister-in-law is a nurse who's on maternity leave with a baby at home. For most of the pandemic, my brother and my mother couldn't see each other because they were both at-risk for different reasons. My grandfather passed away during the first wave in Ontario. I had stayed with him every hospital admission he had until COVID. He didn't pass away from COVID, but he passed away from complications related to his autoimmune disease. I didn't get to spend time with him before he died.

Everyone in my family suffers from some type of autoimmune disease. I wanted to create a safe space for them and for all families who were at risk during this time. I understand it's not easy to create a safe space, but that if I could create this safe space for the pandemic, I could create a safe space for many different events, tragedies, or even routine surgeries.

This is why I started Fero International Inc. It's a modular infrastructure company with a twist. The modular infrastructure industry globally is a $120 billion industry, but it's just at its infancy. What we did first was build the most difficult type of infrastructure we could: hospital infrastructure. We built an ICU room and an operating room out of shipping containers. Once we thought they were ready, we had them tested by the University Health Network in Canada. (The University Health Network is made up of a number of hospitals—one of them being the Toronto General Hospital, which is rated the fourth-best hospital in the world).

The University Health Network wrote a report to us with some feedback, but they gave us the go-ahead to deploy these units. We applied the feedback and then took our systems a few steps further. We've taken our proprietary system, the air system and the pressurization system, and applied it to other indoor spaces: schools, long-term care facilities, remote indigenous infrastructure, military settings, etc. At Fero International Inc., we have the ability to create safe indoor spaces very quickly and cost-effectively, to reach some of the most vulnerable people on earth.

Our infrastructure has the ability to quickly respond to infectious disease like COVID. In our lifetime, we've experienced emergency outbreaks of H1N1, SARS, MERS, swine flu, and bird flu. The current pandemic has forced us to acknowledge that there will be more outbreaks and they will only get more deadly. We acknowledge the importance of safe indoor air, which we've been able to create.

Our units are able to do 30 air changes an hour, twice the amount that the CDC recommends. We can make our units a negative, positive, or neutral pressure depending on their function and who they are serving. Pressurization is a more familiar concept in hospitals, but having a negative pressure environment decreases viral load, and so you can help create safer classrooms. On the long-term care side, we've decentralized the HVAC, so there's no air flow between rooms. We can easily connect our units to an existing long-term care facility to temporarily house someone who has tested positive for influenza or another sort of outbreak. This temporary housing ensures that the rest of the long-term care population doesn't gets sick.

Our units are built with the purpose of increasing hospital capacity very quickly, ensuring that the airflow in the rooms decreases viral load as much as possible, and giving families the opportunity to visit sick people even in an outbreak situation. Even though the company is a year old, we've been contacted by countries all around the world who heard about us through the grapevine. There's a massive movement to support all that we are trying to accomplish. Fero International is much bigger than any business I've started, but truly, I was just upset by COVID-19 and wanted to do something to help.

Believing in Yourself

How did I start and grow a business in the middle of a pandemic that devastated so many? I believed in myself. How did I start another business after years of being an entrepreneur? I believed in myself. There have been periods of time in my career where I lost belief in myself, where the business slowed down, or I didn't have any ideas. In the moments when I lost belief in myself, I didn't work towards my goals in the same way that I did when I believed in myself. I never gave up.

If an entrepreneur tells you they had no tough times, they would be lying. Elon Musk has been on the brink of bankruptcy. Gary Vee has been through hard times. I had a hard day today before I sat down to write this chapter. Serial entrepreneurs all experience setbacks, even if they only choose to share the big wins. Clients don't pay, projects unravel, or we can't raise the money that we thought we could raise. The stock market reacts badly to something out of our control, or a global pandemic shuts down the whole world. There's always something to overcome, and there is an endless number of things that go wrong today, tomorrow, and in five years. But there's also an endless number of things that go right. *That's* what should drive you. I think people sometimes get discouraged as entrepreneurs by the things that could go wrong, but you have to be strong enough to overcome those things and power on until things go right.

I've been a serial entrepreneur for over 10 years, and I still find myself overcoming challenges on a daily basis. Even if you're already successful, you have to continue to believe in yourself and do the work. You have to believe that you can scale from zero to a million, or 10 million to a billion. These are big, big jumps. It takes a lot of work, and you may find yourself feeling like you're starting from scratch again. Entrepreneurship is a constant journey—you have to continue believing in yourself, doing the work, and never giving up.

What Is Success?

We've all seen the quotes from some of the great athletes or inventors who say that they failed 1,000 times to succeed once. They took 10,000 shots before they scored the goal. They did it wrong 100 times before they did it right. Entrepreneurship is about taking those shots. It's continuously taking those shots and being flexible enough to pivot when something goes wrong. You'll hit a wall. You'll face setbacks. You'll have to try something new. But you have to believe in yourself, never give up, and keep trying. Because even those 10,000 shots aren't a failure.

When things go wrong, you don't have to believe that you have failed or that you are failure. Most of the time, you just need to pivot in order to move forward. During COVID, a lot of companies had to pivot, switching the products that they manufactured or learning how to work from home. To me, that change is still a success.

Other strategies can quickly turn a setback into a success. Mentorship can help you improve upon your idea. Mentorship can show you which ideas to abandon and which ideas to pursue. Not everything I've ever tried worked, and I have enough experience to recognize that. But I believe that many of my ideas will work, and all it takes is a pivot of the idea or a little bit of mentorship can assist them to get their idea over the finish line. The point is—you can't give up when you hit these setbacks. Not when you believe in yourself and your success.

Ultimately, success comes in many forms. To me, if the team is aligned, everybody's happy and employed, and the company is still making money, a company is still successful, even if they aren't in line with the original vision of the company. Whether Fero International focuses more on units for hospitals, schools, or military settings, our success is based on my team's alignment and whether or not we are moving forward. I became an entrepreneur because I always want to grow, I always want to invent, I always want to create new products, solve more problems, and create more solutions. And so, if I'm moving in that direction, I would call that a success, fulfilling the belief that I've always had in myself as an entrepreneur and a businesswoman.

Enjoying the Journey
Paul Prior, CEO of GRY. MTTR.

In my DNA is a constant need to share knowledge and help other people. I know I'm not the only one. Some people like to help others through philanthropy or working with charities. I absolutely admire that, but I've never been the person to help in that way. I help in my own way: I've yet to meet a company that I've encountered that couldn't be doing way better than they were doing. And most of the reason that they weren't doing better than they were doing was because they failed to tackle the real issues within it. I help them by identifying the issues and putting together a team that can produce the results that the company is looking for. This is what I do at GRY. MTTR.

My goal is to build GRY. MTTR. off of a six-figure blueprint, but this blueprint doesn't look like the blueprint of the consultancy firms that have come before me. I have my own ways of defining success for myself and my company, and I have my own ways of achieving that success, too.

My experience has taught me that no one's six-figure blueprint is the same. By the time you've built everything in your blueprint, you've probably started thinking about the next blueprint. As entrepreneurs, we are rarely satisfied with the success that we're seeing in our personal and professional lives. We always want more. Of course, building what we sketch out on our blueprints isn't going to be easy. There are going to be some tough times when you desperately need to ask for help even when your pride is telling you otherwise. But learning and growing as an entrepreneur isn't just about reaching six, seven, or eight figures. Learning and growing as an entrepreneur means that you're learning and growing as a person, too.

It's okay to be who you are as you build your business. There's a million ways you can achieve success, however you define it. Don't lose who you are, and don't ever give up.

When Have I Achieved Success?

GRY. MTTR. was a natural next step on my journey as an advisor and an entrepreneur. I spent 20 years traveling the globe working as an advisor with companies all across the board. I worked with Netflix during the early adoption days, Amazon during the one-click processing days, and also with companies like the Road Accident Fund in South Africa. During this time, I realized that the value of the services that I was providing were becoming commoditized. Tier-one consultancy firms were getting smaller but weren't losing the quality of what they provided to clients. Once this clicked, GRY. MTTR. was born.

Being an entrepreneur has given me the opportunity to achieve a few things. First, I get to help the clients that I want to help and solve problems all day. I get to do what I love most about advising, but under my own brand. Second, I'm able to build something that I can eventually hand over to a much stronger and more capable leadership team and have the option to make passive income while still keeping an interest in various projects.

Getting a company to a point where you can confidently hand it over to your team is a lot of hard work, but it's worth it in the long run. My core reason for living is to be the best husband and the best father I can be. I'm not going to die and have a gravestone that boasts about my entrepreneurial ventures. People are going to remember me by the future I created for my kids. Along the way, I can create a better future for my employees and how we approach the workplace, but above everything we're doing at GRY. MTTR. is my family.

When people ask me about feeling successful, I tell them achieving success is giving my family the ability to live the type of life that they want to live. I want my kids to be able to go to the schools they want to go to and to grow up feeling like they are providing value to the world in whatever way they want to do so.

When Has GRY. MTTR. Achieved Success?

This is the drive behind me as an entrepreneur, but of course I need to build a successful business to be able to hand it over and reach my larger goals. The only way that I knew that I had a six-figure company on my hands was that we were able to provide value to companies that were prepared to pay us for our services. Once we had the right pricing strategy and our platform was delivering value, I knew I was on the right path.

When you're measuring success in your business, you only have to focus on three real metrics: revenue, cost and risk. Why overcomplicate things with 160 different metrics when you can just look at your business from a customer's perspective? If our clients are satisfied, and we achieve the results that we promised them, we're successful. This translates to profit because we know what to charge for our services. Measuring success for your business doesn't have to be more complicated than that—that's why we're all planning a *six-figure* blueprint.

Of course, you can also look at the company's mission and work toward succeeding there. GRY. MTTR. was born to support a workforce that wants more flexibility. They want to feel like they're making a difference and achieving success for our clients, but they also want to live their lives and achieve goals outside of work. They want to provide for their families, too. They don't want their job positions to be on their gravestones. Whether they're living in the countryside, in the city, or the far corners of the Earth, we deserve to provide that opportunity to them.

We build these solutions for the employees of our clients but also for our own employees. GRY. MTTR. has employees everywhere you can think of, and none of us works 9-5 days. Each of our employees gets a metric that they need to hit—whether they hit it in two hours or 200 hours doesn't matter to us. We place value on talent as much as we place it on time.

I know that this is unique, but I think we need to shift the way that we look at value from an organizational perspective. We need to change the way we knit all our employees together. We're no longer living in Henry Ford's world. His blueprints are irrelevant, even though so many businesses are still building their workforce around them.

How Do We Get There?

There's an interesting trait that you'll find among entrepreneurs. We all define success differently, but we have one thing in common: we're always thinking about the next thing. I am always surprised to hear people tell me that I'm successful. I never think I am—with every target I reach, I've already set a new target.

Success is about the journey, not a destination. I always want my family to have a better and better life. I always want GRY. MTTR. to make a bigger impact and satisfy more clients. I get a kick out of the journey. Some people become an entrepreneur because they want freedom. Some want financial independence. I like all of these things, but I'm on this journey because of the journey that it's taken me on over the past 20 years. There's so much that you can learn that you just can't access in a corporate environment.

Not every day has been perfect. I've had to learn a lot because I've failed a lot. But I enjoy the lessons I learn from failing. Entrepreneurship is a bit like having kids—there's no degree in having kids. There's no one blueprint for every parent or entrepreneur that can tell you exactly how to build the perfect night. Entrepreneurs should expect lonely nights, tears, fear, and the panic of not having a solution for yourself, your employees, or your clients. But you can also expect waking up the next morning and having the solution come to you in a dream or a meeting. There's always an opportunity to create and learn something new, and that's a wonderful journey to take.

Every year, I reflect on where I am and where I want to go. Every three years, I do a lot of personal development. I look at the skill sets that I have, the type of person I am, and where I am on my journey. And if I feel like I've stepped off the path, which I have many times, I reach out to a mentor or I ask for help. Anyone who has been a mentor to me would say I'm an absolute sponge for feedback. In my personal development work, I've worked very hard to not be defensive when someone's trying to give me advice. When someone gives me advice, I usually take it as the truth, because sometimes we can't see the wood from the trees. If someone has taken time out of their day to tell you something that they think you can improve on, I think it's always valuable to listen to it.

Don't be afraid to ask for help along your journey. I've never had someone turn me down when I've gone to them with a genuine desire to grow and improve. I've never turned someone down when they needed help, either. There's always someone out there that is smarter than you, so find that person and ask for their help. And then pay it back when you've achieved it yourself. That's what makes the journey so enjoyable for me—and whether or not you're close to the metrics you've set for yourself, this willingness to learn and help others will make your journey more enjoyable, too.

Don't Give Up

Asking for help isn't easy. Being an entrepreneur isn't easy. Building a six-figure business from the ground up is going to take a hell of a lot of work. But the only skill you're going to need is resilience. I often say even to clients that we're able to produce results that a lot of companies can't. We can guarantee this because I know that when we're in a boardroom, and everyone in that room except one person is shooting down an idea, we don't just give up along with everyone else. If we believe in an idea, we will convince a second person that we can achieve it. We will convince a third, a fourth, a fifth, until every person in the room is willing to move forward and give the idea a go. We never give up.

People just give up for so many reasons. They don't want their ideas to affect their social relationships. They don't want to sacrifice things for an idea. They don't want to be the only person in the room with a differing opinion. But people without resilience also don't realize that the people who are rooting against them aren't willing to take the journey that's ahead of them. No one's six-figure blueprint is the same. Not everyone is even willing to draw up a six-figure blueprint because they're afraid their plans will never get built. Don't be that person. Draw up your plans and enjoy the journey of building whatever it is that you want to build. Ask for help along the way—and most importantly, don't give up.

From Ideas to Success
Lisa-Nicole Dunne, Managing Director
and Founder of Mantra Strategy

I call myself an idea machine; I'm always coming up with big ideas and encouraging my teams to make them into a reality. My knack for coming up with big ideas has shaped my career, from working with global brands, national brands, and the Children's Medical and Research Foundation.

Some of my ideas come to me in the office, while I'm on a walk, or just when I'm sitting at home. One night while I sat at home, ideas kept coming to me. I decided to bring five sheets of blank paper up to my attic and just wrote everything down. What I thought of that night became Mantra Strategy: I had the business concept, name, model, and high-level business plan all written out in one night.

But there was just one problem—I had a day job. The next day, I went to my day job asking myself if I was brave enough to make the jump to become an entrepreneur. Starting a business can be scary, and having a father who is self-employed, I've seen the pitfalls of going into business on your own. I tucked the idea and the blank sheets of paper away for a couple of months until the pandemic hit.

Fortunately, the pandemic gave me an excuse to exit my day job and try something new. I had an opportunity to think, reflect, and really ask myself what I wanted to do with my career. I've always told people to follow their passion, and now was my time. I started to put the feelers out and talked to people about the idea I had written down on those blank sheets of paper: a high-quality boutique consultancy, all based around experts who work with charities and companies on strategy, leadership, and culture development, with the goal of making an impact.

Mantra Strategy isn't just an advisory; we help organizations really challenge the status quo and come up with a big idea that helps their teams come together and rally. We help them use ideas to do stuff that means something to them, their teams, and their larger mission.

Initially, I felt a little crazy fleeing to my attic with blank sheets of paper; but today, when I look over them, I realize how closely they align to what I'm doing at Mantra Strategy now.

I wonder if I would have taken the jump to start Mantra Strategy if it wasn't for the pandemic—it might have taken me longer to take the plunge. But I know I would have become an entrepreneur at some stage in my life: I follow my ideas. I share them with others. Most importantly, I turn these ideas into a reality. That's what an entrepreneur does.

My ideas were what encouraged me to originally pursue Mantra Strategy, but an idea is just the beginning. In order to turn your idea into a six-figure business, you have to surround yourself with excellent people, know your purpose, and work hard.

Growing, Scaling, and Networking

The timing surrounding Mantra Strategy couldn't have been better. A lot of entrepreneurs tend to take a running start with their business without figuring out the full structure. The business evolves quickly, but the entrepreneur is stuck trying to adjust everything so that it can scale. With the pandemic, entrepreneurs had more time to think, reflect, and prepare their businesses before they launched. I believe that entrepreneurs will be more successful when they can step back, look at their business as a business, set it up to scale, and put together good finance systems and a CRM from the get-go. When you automate more of your business, you can spend your time on the things that will help you define where your business fits in your industry and help you grow.

The answers don't come right away—seeds take a while to grow. If you feel stuck and don't know what the bigger picture looks like, talk to people. Entrepreneurs should engage with people not just when they're looking for things, but also just to keep a good network.

When you have a network ready to support you, you're going to have a much easier time knocking on someone's door for advice or support. From the beginning, people in my network reminded me how important it was to stick with my vision, because I was offering a service that was truly needed and had the potential to help organizations and charities throughout the country. Even in times when I was wobbling and refining the structures that would later become my business model, that support kept me going.

After exiting my last company, I was building Mantra Strategies while taking unemployment checks. The business took off faster than I had expected, but fortunately, I had set the business up in such a way that it would be built for growth and scale. I kind of knew by the feedback I was getting that the business was going to do well, even if it would take a few months. I credit a lot of my success in the early months of starting my company to networking, staying in touch with people, and sharing my vision with them. I've built a strong mission for Mantra Strategy ever since I wrote down the first versions of it on a blank sheet of paper in my attic. During the pandemic, a lot of people were feeling tender and hopeless, and they were excited to buy into the vision that I had set up and brought to them.

Know Your Purpose

The most important ideas I had for Mantra were about its purpose. No matter what type of company you want to start, you have to know your purpose. If companies can really get passionate about doing something and standing for something, from connecting their employees to their personal goals to helping the community, they'll really reap the benefits.

If you are an entrepreneur you have to ask yourself, "What are we all about?" When you have the answer, ask yourself, "Will this propel us forward?" If the answer is yes, keep going.

At Mantra Strategy, we want people to be happier at work, more fulfilled, and more effective and strategic at reaching their goals. We know our purpose. I think it's going to take a little bit of time for us to reach our larger goals because we started in the middle of a pandemic. We started it while we were homeschooling, unable to travel, and not free to do a lot of things that we normally could do to work toward our purpose. But what's important is that we believe in this purpose, no matter how fast we are moving toward it. This larger purpose is something that I want to achieve in and out of the office—so I have the freedom to do it in such a way that works for me and my life.

The purpose of Mantra Strategy aligns with my personal goals. I want to do good, meaningful work and build a company where we can add value to companies, communities, and charities. I want to see good charities become great charities with long-term, sustainable funding options and a much more strategic way and approach to doing work. Through all of this work, I want to build a strong brand with a reputation for good work. I want to see Mantra with a high rate of repeat customers and positive referrals. I want to help as many people and organizations as possible realize their purpose and move toward it. This isn't just an idea that I came up with—it's my passion.

If you want to start a business, do something that you're really, really passionate about. Build something that you believe can help make the world a better place. My purpose drives me through tough times. If you're doing stuff that doesn't really matter to you, or doesn't really make any difference in the world, you're not going to find it easy to kind of push forward and keep working hard.

Regardless of your purpose or your network or how long you've had experience as an entrepreneur, if you want to succeed you have to work hard. Hard work is at the center of any six-figure blueprint. I tell people that Mantra is like a magnet for good people and we're able to do good work and good projects. But even though I'm enjoying every risk that I'm taking and every step of the process, I still have to go through it. I have had to slog to get to where I am today and build up the experience that has made me good at the things that makes Mantra so special. But it's worth not being an overnight success, because every day that I am working hard I am enjoying what I do.

Mantra Strategy has only been live for nine months. We have focused on good quality work, working with really interesting and diverse groups and seeing where our value can be most impactful for organizations. We're already growing, and I think it's because I took the time to build sustainable processes and put our purpose at the core of everything that we do.

It might take a lot of organizations time to find us and come to us; but when they do, we will be ready to help them realize the ideas that got them into business in the first place. That's why I created Mantra Strategy, and that's what I will continue to do long after our blueprints have to be erased and redrawn.

Think About Changing the World
Craig Olson, Worldwide Mobile SteelSeries

Normally, there's a pretty substantial chasm between a good idea for a product or industry and when early adopters are interested in buying into that idea. The vision that I've had for the future of mobile gaming has been my focus for many years; years that I had to patiently wait for the rest of the world to catch up. When you're on the cutting-edge and building a blueprint that seems impossible to carry out, the best ideas feel wrong for a long time until you're right. That was certainly the case for us. I am currently the president of Worldwide Mobile SteelSeries, but even when I was the CEO of Discovery Bay Games, I had a lot to learn about how important it is to stick to the development of an exceptional product. The potential for your success is much larger than you think it is—work at realizing your vision long enough, and you will achieve it.

Eight years ago, WorldWide Mobile was acquired by L Catterton, the world's largest private equity fund investing in consumer-facing companies. L Catterton and I have been talking about the future of mobile gaming for a couple of years; I have been in the gaming industry for close to two decades, and I've been on the cutting edge as the industry has become increasingly mobile. Once L Catterton acquired Steel Series, I was the first senior executive they hired, and my job was to take mobile gaming from a very pre-market concept to kind of the mass-market stage. This is the latest chapter in a much longer journey to my story, and although I thought the path toward success would be much swifter than it actually was, my determination to carry out my vision and provide great products to consumers never wavered.

I started a game company in 2006 with one concept for a board game. When we launched it, we ended up winning Breakout Product of the Year and got national placement in a now-defunct bookstore chain called Borders. The national placement brought us a lot of attention, and we eventually became a best-selling product at Barnes and Noble and other national chains.

And about the same time, Cranium was purchased by Hasbro; Cranium was a Seattle-based board game company that was highly successful at the time. But when Hasbro acquired them, they let their entire development staff go. This was great news for us. All of a sudden, we had the best game development team in the whole country. Even though we had reached a great level of success before, we were just getting started. We developed a bunch of high-profile projects, including Saturday Night Live: The Game, which launched not only in board game format, but later as an iPad app.

To put this into perspective, the launch of the app was when Apple was still in the process of developing the iPad. We met the team at Apple at a conference in New York in very early 2010 and a week later, I took my team to Cupertino. A few months later, we developed a multiplayer game that was used as a demo app on every iPad in Apple stores, to show consumers what the iPad can actually do.

Again, we were just getting started. This was the beginning of a huge partnership with Apple. The game we put on the iPad was a multiplayer game; Apple encouraged us to develop an accessory that would work with iPads and iPhones so everyone could play on multiple devices. We developed the first accessory for the iPad ever in 2010, and we pioneered the first several game controllers that Apple ever approved.

We may take the accessories and abilities that we have now with our Apple devices for granted, but in 2010, we were still pushing the idea that mobile gaming would take hold as much as it has today. Our team saw very clearly that mobile gaming was going to be part of the reason why people would be so addicted to their smartphones. But in those days, people weren't feeling that addiction and didn't pay attention to mobile games. The growth was clearer to us than the rest of the world. Even though there are lots of other things one can do on mobile devices, we saw that, for the most part, people wanted to play games.

It was very clear that our vision was going to become reality over time. Sure, it took longer than we expected. But now, mobile gaming is a dominant form of entertainment and activity on smart devices. Mobile gaming has also overtaken *all* forms of gaming. The funny thing about ideas is that for a long time, an idea might be wrong, but then it's right. A product that was proposed in 2010 might not "make it," or make sense, but when re-introduced to the world in 2020, it's a hit. Remember this as you're building your blueprint.

When you work directly with Apple and Google and you see the reach that they have, you will be humbled immediately. Any CEO realizes that they're not that big of a deal when standing next to these giants. Apple thinks in terms of billions—over a billion people are using their devices every day. They're available in over 100 countries, so when they think about their products, they're thinking about reaching the far corners of the globe. Given that our partners are such big companies and think at such grand scales, my view of reaching others has expanded. I think it's so exciting to meet with someone who has a product that's scalable on an international level. There are no limitations and plenty of opportunities. Those are the blueprints that I want to come across my desk.

But how do you get there in the first place? When I think about this question, I refer back to Apple's philosophy. Apple has the greatest mindset of all, which is to create a great product first. Worry about the consumer experience first. Don't worry about your competition; just make a great product. That perspective is so important. It's all about creating a great product; when you can do that, you can make the world a better place. And that's what it's all about for me.

That's obviously easier said than done. I think one of the most difficult things for anybody to do, irrespective of what they're doing, is to have time for deep, different thinking. We don't have time for contemplative thinking, to step back, look at things broadly, and try and think critically in terms of what the future might hold. This has been true for all of recorded history—we're just working day to day, caught up in the mundane or in the tactical items we have to take care of each day. But if you want to have a vision that will change the world, you need to have the wherewithal or force yourself to find time to think deeply and think differently and think about all of the new products and new services that the world needs. Think about what exists today, what might exist, and to open your mind to what could be. That's the hardest part of being an entrepreneur or a leader, in my opinion. If you can take the time to do that and think about the problems that need to be solved, you'll undoubtedly be successful with whatever you're trying to pursue.

Growing up, I wasn't a complete gaming geek. I learned my most valuable lessons through athletics: I learned how to work really hard and to remain really positive, irrespective of what's around me. Entrepreneurship isn't all international deals and fame. There are moments when your idea is rejected or you have to wait years and years for people to see the vision that you have for your products. When you have an idea or a business, you have to be able to find positivity in any situation and remain calm, irrespective of the storm around you. This mindset has been super helpful—the insatiable drive to keep going toward my objectives, irrespective of everything that might slow me down along the way, has gotten me to where I am in my career.

But I still haven't reached my ultimate objective. One can never, in my humble opinion, ever reach one's objective. For me, there is always going be something else I want to do with my life. I want to do a number of things and make the world a better place in a number of areas. One of my three children is a special needs child who was born with trisomy 21, the most common form of Down Syndrome. My ultimate objective is to find a way to help this really important cause. I want to help not just at a national level, but at the global level. My work is never done.

I was never in the mobile gaming business for the dollar signs. From my perspective, I get up every day and go to work to make the world a better place with great products. This has been my goal throughout my time in the gaming industry. If I can find some way to delight and bring a pleasurable experience to folks around the world with a high quality, well designed, well-built product, I'm happy. I firmly believe that fulfilling whatever the criteria is for a good product, whether it's a long battery life or better compatibility with multiple devices, we do make the world a better place. Games bring people together. They're a way to relax and a way to escape. Whatever we can do to bring about more satisfied customers will bring about a better world. I feel like I've done a good job when I walk into an Apple store, see a live demo of our products, and see new consumers using them for the first time with delight. I feel joy when my kids have their friends over, and I just happen to see that their friends have one of our devices in their backpack. That's what it's all about for me—seeing people have a great time with their family, their friends, or maybe by themselves, playing games, using our mobile devices.

Getting to this point took many years of building, working, and waiting for the right moment when the world would catch onto mobile gaming. But along the way, I've prioritized the products I'm putting out and the people who are using them. This comes before any monetary milestone. If you have an idea, keep this in mind. Make a great product first. If you focus on making a great product and have confidence in your vision, the time it takes for other people to buy in won't matter. The products you make today *could* change the world tomorrow. Think about that.

SCRAP YOUR PLANS AND START AGAIN

Faster than a Hurricane
Brian Diaz, CEO of Pacifico Group

As I write this chapter, I am a few months short of my 28th birthday. And yes, I have built a business that has hit the six-figure mark. I'm the CEO of Pacifico Group, a Puerto Rico-based consultant group that deals primarily with disaster recovery and project management.

Two associates and I started this company when I was just 22 (my associates are close in age). I was finishing up my major at the time, but I didn't want to wait to start a business. Entrepreneurship has always been the path I have walked on.

The business I am running now is not the business that I had envisioned at the age of 22, but that is not surprising to me. Entrepreneurs must understand that, in addition to knowing who they are and what they want their business to be, many things are out of your control. We have seen this with the COVID pandemic. In an instant, things can change. The market you were trying to enter may completely turn on its head within a matter of days or weeks. That's the reality of this lifestyle. You have to learn how to adapt, stay focused, and move forward in the wake of any crisis or surprise; that's the only way that you can continue to grow when everything around you is changing.

Starting a business at 22 didn't feel like a huge mountain to climb. I started my first business at the age of 17—a sales company. As the son of a military veteran and the first of seven children, I always felt a duty to start a business and bring in funds to support my family. And I found success with this mindset early on—within a year of starting my first company, I had a whole team of salesmen below me. My entrepreneurial ways were temporarily put on hold as I worked in a restaurant while working toward my degree, but I knew that sooner rather than later, I would be back in the driver's seat with a new business.

This vision became a reality when I teamed up with Gabriel Gomez and Hiram. Originally, my associates and I had built a platform to help state entities streamline their debt collection. For a bunch of young guys who were still working on their college degrees, we weren't doing too bad. Then, everything changed for us.

As an entrepreneur, you have to understand that there are some things that you can control and some things that you *definitely* cannot control. What you have to do is adapt to the things you cannot control and find a way to come out on top.

We learned this lesson thanks to a natural disaster. In 2017, Hurricane Maria hit Puerto Rico. Everything on the island stopped. We lost all of our customers because the focus was no longer on collecting debt. Public entities needed to give aid, not take it away, and they needed to give aid immediately.

I was 22 at the time, and our business was threatening to go under. But we weren't going to give up without a fight. The disaster recovery market on the island wasn't crowded, which posed an opportunity and a challenge for us. We could bring our expertise to this market and not only survive as a business, but also help people on the island.

As we were exploring what it means to be a leader in such a large company, my team and I had to simultaneously explore the market we were entering. You cannot take your time in the disaster recovery market. People needed help fast, so we had to move fast.

There was no time to think about all of the outcomes—we either came out on top, or we didn't. We needed to make educated guesses and go for it.

Pacifico Group ended up partnering up with another company based out of Maryland to put together a structure for the recovery program on the island. We built a platform that helped local institutions and municipalities get funds from FEMA and other organizations in just one day. Normally, these groups would have to wait three or four weeks for aid—now, they were seeing almost instant results and did not have to wait to provide aid to those in need.

This was the big-time for us. Government bodies could trust us to expedite the recovery process. We started to negotiate big contracts—large-scale negotiations. As we found success, we started not only to manage recovery projects, but also budgeting, compliance and everything regarding public administration as a whole. It was a really big, complicated process, but it has shaped Pacifico Group into what it is today.

Businesses today cannot just focus on projects that will make them money. Money is important, but entrepreneurs should look beyond the dollar signs and see how they can give back to society. What essential services are you providing? What is guiding your business and your individual moral compass? The sense of duty that I felt to my younger brothers and sisters reflects the sense of duty that I feel as an entrepreneur. I believe that this carried us forward as we moved fast and made big changes in response to Hurricane Maria.

You can control the priorities you set for your business—but you can't always control other factors. Hurricanes, health scares, and changes in the market may throw you for a loop. You cannot control how young you are when you start a business or the age and experience of your competitors. Keep moving. Set your priorities, stay focused on them, and you'll be able to navigate anything that hits your business as you grow, expand, and reach that six-figure mark.

In life and in business, there are many distractions that can pull you away from your business. Entrepreneurs may only see certain elements of their business as a short-term priority. They might want to make money before they can accomplish other goals or provide an excellent service before they make a lot of money doing it. No matter what step you are at in your business or how long you plan to be there, you have to know your priority.

When you have a strong sense of your priorities and goals, you can move faster through pivots, growth periods, or just educating yourself about the industry where you want to do business. You don't have to be in emergency response to feel the sense of urgency around you. New niches within every industry create opportunities for entrepreneurs to claim their stake, expand their business, and reach a wider audience. If you don't take advantage of these opportunities, your competitors will.

Moving fast, but staying focused on one goal, helps you achieve that goal much faster. Within 18 months, Pacifico Group was able to hit the six-figure mark. That's a phenomenal timeline—most businesses fail within their first year. But I have to admit, we weren't satisfied with that. Once we hit the six-figure mark, I wanted to hit the seven-figure mark. Once we hit the seven-figure mark, we wanted to hit the eight-figure mark.

I don't want to just hit goals every year—I want to excel. This is our fourth year operating as a company. We are just getting started, but as long as we continue to set goals, focus on them, and move fast, we will excel and expand in ways that we might have never predicted at the age of 23.

If we had waited just a few years to start Pacifico Group, we would have missed the opportunity to enter the disaster recovery space. We would not have been able to help Puerto Rico overcome the hurricane in the ways that we did. Moving fast means that you do not wait. Don't wait to reach your 30s or finish your degree. If you want to start a business, start a business. Do not wait, and do not be discouraged by other factors that are outside of your control.

Because I started my business at 23, I can say at the age of 27 that I am running a business that is well beyond the six-figure mark. If you want a six-figure business in one, two, or five years, start now.

We want young entrepreneurs to know that you do not have to wait until you are in your 30s or 40s to start a business. Move fast—even though you are young, you have a lot to contribute. Yes, other people in the industry will be older than you or have more experience in certain spaces. Disregard that. Experience and age are nothing if you cannot deliver a productive solution or serve your clients well. At any age, use your skills to solve the problems affecting your communities and don't be afraid to push your way into a market that has room for you.

If the market appears to be dominated by giants, look closer. We want small businesses to know that you do not have to shy away from big corporations in your industry. Clients will come to you if you consistently deliver better service and results than the larger names who are more focused on cutting costs than solving problems. Don't focus on the budgets and the recognition that these other companies have. If you have something unique that you can give to people, you can make money off of it. Do not limit what you put on your blueprint.

It's Not About the Dollar Figure
Izabella Roth,
CEO of Infinity Healthcare Ltd.

S tarting a business is scary, but you can't grow as a human until you start doing things that scare you. And if you start a business for the right reasons, and with a kind heart, it can be one of the best things that you do for you, your family, and your community.

I'm the CEO of Infinity Healthcare, a provider based in Edmonton, Canada. I'm a registered nurse by background with 15 years of experience in home care. But I knew deep down that there was more for me and more for Alberta in terms of home care experiences available. I started my business because I saw a need in the community. We've flown past the six-figure mark, and it's because I believe that the blueprint for success requires kindness, exceptional customer service, and a little bit of creativity.

About Infinity Healthcare

Before I started Infinity Healthcare, I was working in a national private healthcare company. Private healthcare is still a very new industry in Canada since free healthcare is available, and the company where I worked was at the risk of closing down when I started working there. Our revenue was very low for our size—close to $180,000 a year. In three years after my arrival, we increased our revenue to $8,000,000, growing by 2,799 percent.

During this time, I was able to play around with corporate money, experiment with different marketing strategies, and really get familiar with the private healthcare industry. But after a while, I felt that I didn't want all of my efforts to go back to the corporate headquarters up in Toronto. I'm based in Edmonton; I wanted to start a home care company here, so I took the leap in August 2020 and started Infinity Healthcare to bring high-quality home care to Alberta. By December 1 of that year, we had five to six employees in Edmonton. By the end of the month, that number grew to 80, and they were serving customers all across the province.

August 2020 was at the height of the pandemic—a crazy time to start a company, but it was a time where people began to realize that they desperately wanted our services for themselves and their families. We were fulfilling a need that many people didn't know they had until we came along, and that's why we've been so successful.

The Grey Wave

Our world is experiencing a "grey wave." A lot of baby boomers are aging. We're starting to see that there's not going to be enough space in retirement communities for everyone to age comfortably. COVID only made this worry more urgent; people don't want to send their parents or check themselves into retirement communities that are congregate living sites. If a pathogen is easily transmittable, it can spread so quickly throughout our retirement communities and prevent people from spending quality time with their parents and grandparents.

Even before COVID, the grey wave encouraged people to lean into the idea of "aging in place" and staying at home as long as possible. In the long run, even with renovations to make their home more accessible, aging in place actually *saves* people money. An average retirement community costs $7,000-$8,000 a month; with businesses like Infinity Healthcare, it's cheaper to pay for private care at home.

The quality of care also increases with private home care. If your parent is starting their dementia journey, they're going to prefer to be around rooms, furniture, and pictures that are familiar to them. People decline much faster if they move into a new place.

I've seen this with my own eyes many times, at work and at home. My grandmother is in long-term care right now. While we're in lockdown, everyone who visits her at the facility must wear full PPE. I have to wear full PPE. It's scary for everyone involved. None of this would be necessary if she was being treated privately, in her home.

Trends in the market aside, it's people like my grandmother who inspired me to start Infinity Healthcare and elevate the care that people are receiving in the last years of their life. This is why we are so successful. At Infinity Healthcare, we're in it for the right reasons. We're trustworthy and we're honest, and there's no hidden agenda.

Personality Matching at Infinity Healthcare

One of the reasons why we hit the six-figure mark so fast is we do something that no other company here does: personality matching. Part of our process is meeting with customers to assess what they *really* want in a home care professional. If a customer only speaks Italian, then we're going to find a caregiver that speaks Italian. If they enjoy arts and crafts, we'll find a caregiver who is happy to stay a while and knit or crochet with them.

This is unheard of in the Canadian healthcare system. Customer service in healthcare does not exist here. Hospital employees are unionized and don't have to go the extra mile to serve their patients. Home caregivers cycle in and out—someone new might be coming to visit a patient every day. Not only is this a lower quality experience, but it can take away from the precious time that caregivers have with the patients. When someone new is coming in every day, they have to spend a lot of precious time learning about the patient's routine, their medication, their quirks, and everything that contributes to the quality of the patient's experience.

We believe in continuity of care, which is why it's so important that personality matching works. And it does; we haven't lost a single client to bad customer service yet. We do monthly satisfaction calls with the client and the employee to assess the relationship between the two. Staff are genuinely happy and perform better when they love what they do.

Outside of the logistics of the business or the efficiency of the process, personality matching allows our staff and customers to form strong relationships. Our clients have found purpose as they enter their dementia journey thanks to our staff. One client in particular has started knitting, and we matched her with a staff member who knits as well. Together, they make hats for babies in the NICU. This is what we consider a success in our business—not a dollar figure.

Customer Service Is All It Takes

Six figures are important to keep a company going, but what's more important to me is that the staff and the clients are happy.

My motto for the entire company is to bring back customer service to healthcare in Canada. And I don't have to do a lot to make this happen and change someone's day for the better. We had a client who wanted to die a beautiful death at home. When we got to know her, we learned that one of her favorite things to do was play Dungeons and Dragons. Through personality matching, we found nurses who love Dungeons and Dragons, had even played with this patient in a league at one point. For one of our patient's last meals, we set up a Thanksgiving dinner for free from a local restaurant who wanted to help. It was one of the last meals she ever had with her family. These experiences are priceless. They're invaluable. The relationship that these nurses have with the patient's family, even after she has passed, is invaluable.

I don't know how our recruiters do it. I'm a terrible recruiter—I would hire everyone because I love everyone. But our recruiters will call 70 or 75 caregivers for one client, then somehow narrow their choices down through formal interviews to find the perfect match. And this process is disrupting our healthcare system—right now, the government just provides the caregiver by who is available that day.

We're also disrupting how people see their jobs in healthcare. At our orientations, we tell our staff that customer service is all it takes. The benefits they get from that customer service show. A lot of our caregivers don't leave to go home right at four o'clock; they take the extra time to get a cup of tea or do some housekeeping. It's a good system that simply can't be measured in dollars and cents, even though it has an impact on client satisfaction, retention, and referrals.

Growth Through Marketing and Other Means

Our success comes from many things: the timing of the COVID pandemic, our commitment to customer service, and my past experiences in home healthcare. When I talk to entrepreneurs, I don't tell them to expect the same rate of success right away. It usually takes two years for startups to reach any metric of success that you set for yourself. We got lucky that we opened during COVID and COVID made the entire world realize staying at home is the best place to be.

One last strategy that has made us successful is that we've gotten creative. I had the money at my previous position to take risks—I saw what worked. I saw that quirky ideas worked to bring attention and customers to a private healthcare business. I saw that exceptional customer service, whether that means setting up a Dungeons and Dragons game for a patient or calling a restaurant to provide a Thanksgiving dinner, works. People hear our stories, and they hear how genuine our business is—that works.

Print media isn't our thing—we prefer to tell our story in other ways. Before COVID, I sponsored galas for different fundraisers and research societies. I gave speeches with personal stories and stories from the field. These events allowed me to reach a captive audience of 800 to 1,000 people—after every one, my previous company saw an increase of 20-30 percent in revenue.

COVID has made this marketing strategy less accessible now, but the relationships I made through those events carried over when I started Infinity Healthcare. The networks and relationships I had built before I was an entrepreneur helped me when I became an entrepreneur. I believe in the power of networking and nurturing relationships. You should never leave one single relationship in a bad spot.

Just because COVID has put a hold on galas doesn't mean that I can't continue marketing, and it doesn't mean I can't continue taking risks with my marketing strategies. This year, we just sponsored a movie. The movie is about a man that's starting his dementia journey, so we will get some product placement out of our sponsorship. Once the movie has been created, we're going to submit it to film festivals. I'm taking a risk, but the risky, creative marketing strategies have worked. This film is going to be played in people's homes and start a conversation about private home care.

Will this take our revenue from six to seven figures? We'll find out soon enough. But at the end of the day, reaching those numbers is just about funding our mission and allowing us to provide the care that we want to provide for our patients. Dollar numbers may be the metric you use to define success, and that's okay. But don't let the dollar numbers hold you back from letting your best intentions shine through. Starting a business is a risk. Putting customer service above all else in an industry where customer service is readily ignored is a risk. Crazy marketing strategies are a risk. But when you do all of these things with good intentions, your risks are more likely to be rewarded, *and* the risks will be worth it, every step of the way.

Walking Ahead
Mariella M. Dellemijn,
Director of CRM Excellence

Sometimes people ask me if I think I made the wrong decision to study physical education before studying business. They are surprised to learn that I was a physical education teacher before starting a CRM software business. I know that being a PE teacher is not usually on a six-figure blueprint—my father, who worked in business his whole life, was not supportive of my first career path and was relieved when I pivoted to entrepreneurship. But I do not regret this first career path. Studying physical education was the best education I could have ever received. In the first few years of my career, before I considered entrepreneurship, I was able to learn so much that I apply to my businesses every day. I learned about my flaws, my strengths, how to deal with defeat, and how to work in a team. When you know how to organize a group of teenagers, break up their fights, and celebrate victories with them, being a leader in business is much less intimidating.

I might have continued my career in physical education for many years if it weren't for one thing: I didn't want to be stagnant. Finding a teaching job in Holland is not easy, so I had already started studying business before I even had a full-time job at a school. I enjoyed my time as a teacher, but I realized in my studies that I'm too much of an adventurist and an entrepreneur to be stuck in the same job for 20 years. There aren't many options to advance your career if you are a physical education teacher. I decided that I would much rather do something else where I can continue to pivot, grow, and try something new.

This is a theme that has continued to shape my businesses and my careers. I am a person who is always exploring and thinking ahead. Most of the time, I am thinking too far in the future, so I have put together a team that knows how to organize all the ideas, good and bad, that I am exploring day to day. I'm not great with getting into the details or administrative concerns of each of my ideas, but that is what my team is for. Everybody has their strengths—and because I know mine, I have been successful in business.

Not every idea that you have as an entrepreneur will be viable, but if you are building a strong business with a strong team, you have to be able to walk ahead, gain experience, and brainstorm ideas that will transform your business in the future. If this is not something that you enjoy doing, you may not be an entrepreneur. But if you do like to walk ahead, this might be the career path for you.

After I stopped teaching physical education, I started a CRM software company with my husband. We were based in the Netherlands, but we also had built branches in the United States, Spain, Germany, and Australia. In 10 years, we grew very fast. This was over 20 years ago— "CRM" had not even been a term that was used in our business until 1995. But in 1995, Gardner developed this term because *they* saw the potential of it. What was once "relationship management" or "opportunity management," limited to regional markets, was going to become a global market. In two to five years, Garnder predicted, there would be a few, global players that would dominate CRM software.

After many years of being in business, with the potential to be one of those global players, my husband and I had to make a decision. Did we want to commit to being a global player, or did we want to stick with being a niche player, servicing businesses and organizations throughout Holland?

We chose the first option. We had an IPO, which helped us to grow at an even more accelerated pace. But we found out quickly that we did not like running a huge, global company, and we would prefer to be business owners of a much smaller, more manageable group. In 1999, we decided to sell the company and try something new. I started CRM Excellence with three of my former colleagues that same year. Instead of developing CRM software, we wanted to take our knowledge and experience of the industry and help our customers to make their CRM investments profitable.

That's exactly what we did until 2010. We were able to continue growing as more and more businesses were introduced to, and invested in, CRM. But everything changed in 2010. Social media became the talk of the digital world, although it wasn't quite used for marketing at that time. I was thinking ahead, as I tend to do. I wanted to see whether or not social media would turn out to be something disruptive to the customer relationship management domain, even though I wasn't completely sure if it would be. Some thought that social media was just something for personal use; the youth would use it to share photos and have conversations, but that was as far as it would go in terms of impact. We guessed differently. These conversations had the potential to impact and influence customer behavior. Businesses had the potential to use social media to understand their customers and target groups better. And that's not to mention the potential for social media advertising and other forms of content creation.

When we first guessed that social media could be disruptive to our industry, we started a subsidiary with the goal of simply finding out whether or not social media would only impact the youth or have the potential to impact how people do business as a whole. Our guess was correct, so we changed the subsidiary's name to Fueld and entered into the digital marketing field. From that moment on, CRM Excellence and Fueld would join force on many projects. The same customers who had questions about their investment in CRM often had questions about their investment in social media. They also wanted to integrate the two and build a more comprehensive marketing process that included the digital and physical worlds.

Very quickly, we saw that Fueld was going to stay. Social media marketing wasn't, by any means, going to be a fad. Even back in 2016, I believed that integrating these two businesses would be key to helping B2B businesses with their goals in and out of marketing. Other companies did too; by 2019, other online tools were being developed to help customers accomplish the same goals that we were helping them achieve. It was clear that any business who wanted to dominate needed to invest in these tools and create a strategy that included CRM and digital marketing. If we could provide them with this strategy and solution, we could dominate, too.

Today, we provide our customers with what we call a "marketing solution," where all the aspects and knowledge of digital marketing and CRM are integrated. Our customers can access all of our knowledge and tools for a monthly fee; we provide them with a whole team to add to their own marketing and CRM team. I am still the CEO of both CRM Excellence and Fueld. In practice, we are the same company, and in the near future we will *be* only one company, but we still have two propositions and two pieces of the market.

Ten years after social media was introduced to the world, businesses are still just learning about the potential of this phenomenon and how it can impact their business. Unfortunately, this ten-year gap leaves them behind much of their competition. The companies that saw the potential for these online tools earlier had a much bigger advantage. There is no longer an excuse to ignore social media. Even companies that let mid-level employees handle these strategies are starting to understand that marketing and CRM are strategies that must be discussed by the boards and the higher-ups. These strategies influence how a business organizes their commercial process. Companies who haven't invested this much time, thought, and money into these solutions are finally coming around, albeit too late for many.

The lessons that many businesses have learned from social media can be applied to many areas of business and entrepreneurship. Every entrepreneur is different, but in order to succeed in business for over 30 years, they have to be willing to regularly reinvent the value they bring to their business and their customers. Business moves so fast—sticking to the same ways of doing things and the same mindset does not help anyone. Very quickly, staying the same makes you behind the curve. Entrepreneurs should enjoy their journey, but also be willing to change what they're doing regularly.

The best way to do this is to allow yourself to walk ahead of the crowd. Entrepreneurs are visionaries. They see things that many people do not see or cannot even grasp. That's not a new problem; visionaries have always dealt with people who do not see their vision or follow them fast enough. In order to be the person that people *eventually* follow, you have to walk ahead. You cannot get people to walk or to follow through words—you have to act and walk ahead on your own.

This is scary. People may be tempted to take it personally when others do not follow them or, worse, tell them that their idea is crazy. No one wants to hear that they have crazy ideas or that the path they're walking is a dead-end. If you want to be an entrepreneur and find the path to success, you have to be stronger than that and walk ahead anyway. If we had believed the people that said that social media was just a phase or that it was not going to have an impact on businesses and marketing, we would be nowhere near where we are today.

If you have a crazy idea, pursue that crazy idea. Walk ahead. Crazy ideas aren't just fun to follow—they may also be profitable. Crazy ideas become inspiring ideas. Inspiring ideas become good business ideas. In order to create, build, and grow a successful business, you have to change, and you have to have some crazy ideas. Some of them will work and some will not. Not all paths lead to success. But if you do not follow them and walk ahead on the paths that you want to take, how will you know where they lead?

Know Your Why
Jean Paul Laurent,
Founder and CEO of Unspoken Smiles

I f you told me 10 years ago that my non-profit would have just reached six figures, I wouldn't have believed you. Ten years ago, I had a very specific blueprint for my life; I was going to graduate from dental school, open my own practice, start making six figures, and become one of the many success stories of resilient Haitian immigrants. Starting a nonprofit was not part of my blueprint. But the blueprint you take with you at the beginning of your journey is not always the one that you hold onto ten, 15, or 20 years later. That is okay, as long as your journey is one of learning, believing in your mission, and sticking to your "why."

In 2008, I started school at the NYU College of Dentistry. The journey had already been tough. Every time I entered a classroom, I had to prove myself. I moved to the United States at an older age than many immigrants. Whether I was applying for colleges or seeking funding for my nonprofit, I was competing with younger minds who had achieved so much success in a shorter amount of time.

But I was doing well at NYU, and I was on track to graduate from dental school and open up my own private practice. Then, in 2010, a major earthquake hit Haiti. The disaster destroyed my home. I had to do something to help the people that I loved so much.

When I first planned to travel back to Haiti after the earthquake, I didn't have any money. The only thing I had was the knowledge that I had gained at school. The least I could do was ask a few people for some toothbrushes to help out the kids that I would meet during my trip.

What I realized during that trip changed my life. When I gave the children the toothbrushes and other gifts I had collected, I received a smile in return. I realized that there was so much behind those smiles. Each child had a story to tell. Yes, that story might have the devastation of the earthquake or the poverty that many Haitians face. But those smiles also tell an unspoken story of resilience, of reclaiming power, of leading a new generation in the world's first Black-led republic. I knew that I wanted the world to see these unspoken smiles, that these unspoken smiles could change the world.

And so, instead of continuing on the path to dental school, I went to Columbia University and got my master's in public administration. In 2014, I launched Unspoken Smiles, and I am still the CEO of the organization today, bringing access to quality dental care to people around the world.

Operating Like a Business

Unspoken Smiles may be a nonprofit, but it has a social enterprise aspect to it. We don't aim to grow our profits but to grow the amount of people and communities that we serve throughout the world.

When we looked into the data before Unspoken Smiles launched, we saw that Americans consume a lot of dental care products. They are investing a lot of money in dental health, whether it's for whitening, purchasing toothbrushes, or cosmetic procedures. It's a multi-billion-dollar industry, which means that dental care and oral health are clearly important to people in the United States.

Of course, I already knew how important dental care was to people around the world. As I did more research, I saw just how overlooked dental care is; nearly half of the world population is suffering from dental disease. This is due to many factors: people do not have access to care, they don't know when to seek dental help, or they just simply don't care about it. Fortunately, dental disease is 100% preventable, and by addressing the lack of access to care we can help eliminate dental disease throughout the world.

At Unspoken Smiles, we believe that we can use a business model to promote good and tap into the goodwill of average Americans.

By educating Americans, who understand the importance of dental health, and encouraging them to support the mission, we can create a stable source of funding and provide care.

Every entrepreneur has this sort of hope when they start out. They believe in their mission, but encouraging everyone else to join them often proves to be a challenge. Donors get burned out. They keep getting the call to write a check and eventually get tired by hearing the same story over and over again. Reaching that six-figure level, for us, wasn't going to happen overnight if we stuck to the same old fundraising strategies. So lately, we have adjusted how we generate funding. We created products that people can use and feel proud to wear. These products range from items that we can sell—like a t-shirt—to items that we were previously buying from businesses—like a toothbrush. By creating our own toothbrush and selling it, we have been able to increase our revenue and marketing in one move. A few years later, this move has been paying off. We hit the six-figure mark and we expect to grow even more over the next couple of years.

Reaching six and seven figures in revenue has always been important for me. I've followed the lead of entrepreneurs in the for-profit world so that we could meet new people, travel to new places, and increase impact. We need people in the for-profit world to invest in us just as much as we need government agencies to give us access to key resources. I urge all successful entrepreneurs who want to take their mission to the next level to really embrace public-private partnership and take it from there. Even if you run a nonprofit, you can still launch an apparel company to support your mission.

Know Your Why

Recently, when I was traveling to Haiti, I got into a major car accident. I almost died. And that moment, I started questioning everything. Why was I back in Haiti? Why was I running a nonprofit? Why wasn't I on the path that I had set out on when I first moved to the United States? I called my father, and he told me to remember my "why." He told me to follow my heart. When I looked to my heart, I saw the mission that is behind Unspoken Smiles. My "why" is because I want to place a toothbrush in every child's hand around the world and help them receive access to quality dental care.

It doesn't matter what is on your blueprint, whether you are starting a nonprofit or you are running a business. You have to know your "why." If you don't know why you're working so hard or sacrificing so much, you will fail.

The path to six figures is not straightforward. There are ups and downs. As you navigate this path, you'll encounter many forks in the road and options to bow out of your company. When you know your "why," you're much less likely to quit. When you know your "why," you're much more capable of facing challenges with a fighting spirit.

Really examine your "why." There are so many entrepreneurs who are starting companies or organizations because they want to copy the success of another person. They see someone being successful and they want that success for themselves. That's not good enough—they don't have the "why." People who start businesses based on another person's "why" will not last very long.

Find Someone to Believe In You

Challenges will arise immediately after you start a business. People will look at your blueprint and tell you that they don't think you will succeed. Having a "why" will help you look past the doubts of others, but I also recommend finding someone who believes in you and your idea.

My father supports the idea of Unspoken Smiles, but at the beginning, he didn't understand my "why." I had previously written up a foolproof blueprint that took me on a path through dental school and opening up a private practice—this was something that both of my parents could get behind. When I threw it all away to start a nonprofit, they were hesitant. They weren't the only ones, either.

People will doubt you. People will tell you that you are a failure and you should quit while you're ahead. You need someone to believe in you in order to push forward and prove everyone wrong. Once you receive that validation, it will pave the way for more people to understand your vision and believe in you, too.

In the past couple of years, Unspoken Smiles has received that validation. We had a partnership with Lay's. We had a partnership with Thomson Reuters and the United Nations. I received seed funding from a fellowship. All of these partnerships and validations happened because someone believed in my "why." And that started with me, but the sooner you can get someone to believe in your "why," the easier it will be to move forward.

To be honest, I have had doubts. I sometimes cried at night because I didn't know what's going to happen and what the future of Unspoken Smiles looked like. But every single time I reached my lowest point, I was able to turn to my "why" and to the people that believed in me. I was able to envision the impact that our programs were having and will continue to have in people's lives. That's what has kept me going—not money or status or anything else.

When I started this organization, I had people who reached out to me and said, "Early on, as a kid, I fell and lost my two front teeth. I was embarrassed. I couldn't eat. Until this day, it affected my self-esteem. But organizations like yours helped me get my two front teeth back. And I really appreciate it." This is my "why." And hearing stories like this has kept me moving forward and making this new blueprint of mine come to life.

We Will Never Stop Learning

Today, Unspoken Smiles is operating in eight countries across the world, including India, Romania, El Salvador, Guatemala, Haiti, and Costa Rica. As we expanded to make a more global impact, we embraced the idea that we would always have to learn something new about the impact we are making and the issues that we are addressing. Our care in Haiti has to be completely different from the care we are providing in India, for example, because the people we are working with live in a different culture. They have a different diet and live in a different environment.

We never wanted to create one single approach, but instead to take into consideration the way people are living and the cultures that influence their dental health and everyday lives. We couldn't just come to a country and say, "Hey, we are Americans. We use Colgate, and that's what you have to use." That is not who we are. We are not an organization that gives out freebies to make ourselves feel better. We are dedicated to bringing people their dignity and making their lives better. In order to do that, we have to know how we can make their lives better.

As an entrepreneur, you have to be dedicated to learning every single day. Every time you reach a new horizon, there's always a new horizon behind it that requires new knowledge and new insights. With each country that we expand to, there is more to learn. With each service that we provide, there is more to learn. Opening ourselves up to learning every day is what will make Unspoken Smiles successful on a global stage.

We have programs in Iraq and India. There are people who wouldn't choose to enter these countries because of stereotypes or limited amounts of information, but we have children there who need our help. Our experiences there have taught us so much *and* given us the opportunity to teach other people something new about these countries. There are children in India who are happy to invite us into their home, touching my knees as a sign of good luck. When I go to these countries with an openness to learn and I interact with these children, I've found myself becoming a better leader and a more grounded individual. This allows me to support my mission much more effectively.

Every degree I earn, every trip I take, and every new thing that I learn is worth it because it helps to support our mission of providing dental care to people around the world. I am committed to learning every day as a way to support my "why." I am committed to learning every day as a way to thank the people who have believed in Unspoken Smiles from the start. By having the courage to throw out my old blueprint, I have been able to prove so many people wrong and help everyone in the world engage in the universal language of smiling.

Keep an Eraser Nearby
Jennifer Stasiewich,
Managing Partner at PureInvest Inc.

For someone who studies and plans everything, I surprised myself when I reflected on my journey and realized that I *didn't* have a blueprint for my career or the companies that I'm running now. I've always tried to think *just* a few steps down the road—for many entrepreneurs who embrace the persistence and adaptation that goes along with this lifestyle, that's all you can do to move yourself closer to your definition of success. If the past two years have taught us anything, it's that the farther you plan down the road, the more likely it is that you'll have to change your plans.

Through using what I know about entrepreneurship and business, I want to share the tools that you need to build a six-figure blueprint—one "room," "wall," or "floor" at a time.

About PureInvest

I'm the Founder and Managing Partner of PureInvest. We work with early-stage technology companies across Canada and the United States in a number of different sectors. This wasn't part of my plan when I graduated 11 years ago, but as I worked in the capital markets space, I noted a dearth of institutional capital and support for up-and-coming entrepreneurs in Canada, particularly at the earliest stages of their development. That needed to change. After the bank had backed my first startup, I decided to run with the opportunity and create PureInvest. Now, we work to support financial technology companies, real estate tech companies, health tech companies, and consumer tech companies in similar ways.

I decided to follow through with PureInvest because I knew this business had six-figure potential immediately. During my time on the trading floor at TD Securities, I got to understand the size and the scope of the venture capital world and the number of entrepreneurs who are constantly trying to get off the ground. The venture capital world is truly limitless area to explore, and there are entrepreneurs out there who need help. One day, I could be developing a strategy with a financial technology company aiming to help people manage their money better, and the next day I'm helping to raise capital for a health tech company set out to change the world. There is no one set blueprint to choose from—I get to draw them myself.

What Will Make a Business Successful?

PureInvest looks over a handful of different startups, but my main focus right now started as a passion project. Somm is a wine technology company that pairs consumers with wine—essentially, the Somm app gives consumers a sommelier in their pocket. Although Somm started as a blend between two of my passions (entrepreneurship and wine,) we quickly saw that it had all of the elements of a successful business.

At PureInvest, we look at three different types of metrics to determine whether a business has the potential of drawing up a six- (or seven-, eight-, or ten-) figure blueprint. First, we want to know whether the market wants or needs this business. Everything is a supply and demand equation in some way, shape, or form.

We asked ourselves: Do consumers want this? Do consumers want an app where they no longer have to guess what kind of wine to buy, or what they're going to like from their palate perspective, or where they should be buying? And by looking at the market we determined yes, consumers do want that. Consumers want to stop pretending to know what they're doing when it comes to the wine market. Consumers are also telling us that they want to discover new merchants and products. They want to get to know their own palates better and kind of shop according to their own personal preferences. So, the answer to our first question was a resounding "yes."

Then, we look to determine whether the suppliers can provide what consumers are looking for. Again, we saw that the answer was "yes." We have B2B partners, including restaurants, hotels, wineries, and now agencies knocking on our door to work with us. Clearly, there's demand from the other side of the market that we need in order to make this work.

As a company gets attention, we also look at a third set of metrics. We ask ourselves, "Is the media liking this?" At Somm, we've earned a lot of really great earned media spots. We've been featured on Yahoo's list of top women-run companies that they love; our company has been written up by multiple international outlets, and we're creating a lot of buzz around our technology. Yes, yes, and yes.

I've always known that Somm had six-figure potential. But for me, the success that I see for Somm has more to do with the human value that it's bringing to the market. Obviously, the dollars can make or break whether a company makes an impact on people, but the companies at PureInvest are really about positively impacting people's lives. I believe that Pure Invest is successful because I'm happy with the work that I'm doing and seeing the company grow. I really enjoy building something that's sustainable. After two years of being hit hard, companies like Somm are able to give the hospitality industry some hope and momentum that they desperately need.

Somm is really coming at an opportune moment in time—I think is filling a lot of great voids in the market. But in addition to timing, we've done our research. We've kept track of how each addition to Somm's "blueprint" and the market at large is affecting the company. These changes will only continue to shape the future of Somm as the world continues to adapt to the "new normal" and the digital lifestyles that consumers have become accustomed to living.

Drawing Your Blueprint One Step at a Time

When I first started PureInvest in 2016, we had a much different model than we do now. We focused a lot more on curating cherry-picked networking events where half of the room was up-and-coming entrepreneurs and startups, and the other half of the room was institutional capital providers that could partner or financially back these entrepreneurs. Four years later, COVID hit. We obviously couldn't really do things in the same way, and that's where we started to see more of PureInvest's current model really take shape. Essentially, our model is closer to a boutique consultancy for early-stage tech companies. We still have a great network that we spent the first few years of our lifetime building, but we've naturally had to evolve because the market evolved, and the environment changed.

Our new business model had to prepare for the pivot because things have been so uncertain. But this isn't just a lesson to apply in case of a global pandemic. Markets change. The world changes. Your life will change, whether you are starting your entrepreneurship journey at 22 or considering a career change at 52. You have to be ready for those changes—you have to draw your six-figure blueprint one step at a time *and* be prepared to make changes as you go along.

All entrepreneurs who are looking at empty blueprints need to be comfortable operating in a space of ambiguity and a little bit of discomfort. You can't draw out a blueprint and expect everything to go to plan. Entrepreneurship is not building a house. If you're looking for a predictable routine or a predictable pattern, you're going to have a really hard time adjusting to the entrepreneurial lifestyle. But this doesn't have to be discouraging. I often advise students, young professionals, and even older professionals to give themselves a chance to be uncomfortable. If you haven't let yourself down in the past, you're probably not going to this time. You can operate in a bit of a gray area or ambiguity, feeling the discomfort of not knowing what to "draw" on your blueprint next. A lot of times, entrepreneurs will find that they'll just have to roll up their sleeves and get scrappy. Being ready for that commitment to the roller coaster of entrepreneurship is something that I think aspiring entrepreneurs need to realize and wholeheartedly embrace. It's okay to trust yourself to do your very best. Once you have that trust and you have the ability to change course when you realize that what you're doing isn't working anymore, you'll crush it.

Are You Ready for Entrepreneurship?

I'm not going to sugarcoat the experience of being an entrepreneur. It can be very stressful. Most startups fail, and the ones that do succeed aren't overnight successes. The tech darlings that we take for granted now—Uber, Airbnb, etc. —all struggled to get off the ground. Every entrepreneur has had a door slammed in their face. Every great company has been doubted or rejected. We all have to go back to their plans and change everything to adapt to the market, to a global pandemic, or to our budgets. The leaders that have succeeded and built six-figure businesses, however, are ones that have really thought about *why* they want to be an entrepreneur. This is a journey I took when I started PureInvest, and it's one that I recommend to anyone who is considering taking the leap to become an entrepreneur or make any sort of change in their life.

First, you have to think about the lifestyle that you really want and what's going to make you happy. When you have that idea nailed down, you'll be able to filter out some career aspirations or journeys that you might otherwise choose to take. Once you've figured out the lifestyle you want, you might be surprised as to what career options you have left to potentially pursue.

The second component is figuring out what you're passionate about and your natural talents. Contemplating these things cannot be done overnight—you have to really spend time on this second component and be honest with yourself about what you're good at doing. When you spend your energy, resources, and time on something that you are naturally wired to excel in and you naturally gravitate towards, you're going to end up doing a much better job and not feel like you're working 16 hours a day, seven days a week. (And if you are going down the entrepreneurship track, you *will* be working 16 hours a day, seven days a week, sometimes for years on end).

As you ask yourself all of these questions—about the market you're dealing with, about the lifestyle that you want to create for yourself—your answers might surprise you. That's okay. Building a six-figure blueprint is not about getting it right the first time. As you take the next steps in your life, keep an eraser nearby and focus on one "room" at a time.

Setting your Soul on Fire
Shelley Willingham,
Founder of Vision and Passion
International

Vision and Passion International is not my first company. Around 2001, while I was in my early 30s, I started a company that focused on helping other companies market more effectively to multicultural consumers. I worked with Allstate, Meryll Lynch, and GE, helping them take a look at how much money they were leaving on the table because they weren't marketing effectively (or marketing using tired stereotypes) to different minority groups.

The business was going really well. We grew to 15 employees, I was in *Fortune* Magazine, and life was fantastic. I was believing my own press—so I didn't know how quickly I would fall.

When the market tanked in 2007, one of my largest clients got bought out. I held onto my business for as long as I could because I didn't want to let down the 15 people on my team who trusted me. I cashed out my retirement and stopped paying myself to pay them until there was just no money left and I ended up losing everything that I owned. Within a few years, I went from *Fortune* magazine to having to get food stamps to feed my children. The dream house that I had built with my spouse at the time was taken away. I went from being on top of the world to just trying to get through to the next day.

I couldn't roll out a blueprint and start another business during this time, even though I knew I was born to be an entrepreneur. During that time, I did a lot of soul searching, and I decided that whatever I did next, it would be purely things that set my heart on fire. Vision and Passion came as a result of this mindset shift.

Vision and Passion started as a coaching business, helping entrepreneurs and small business owners. In my soul searching, I was able to put together materials and reflect on my experiences in order to tell clients how to build a company from nothing. I also tell them what mistakes not to make. My clients know all of the experiences that shaped me when I lost everything—learning from my mistakes has helped them avoid detours and shorten the path to success with the tips, strategies, and advice.

Once again, the business grew quickly; I didn't have to do much advertising at all. From that revenue, I started the digital marketing firm. I'm also working on a program right now focused on helping women feel comfortable in their own skin and understand that we can be both pretty and powerful at the same time. Most recently, I joined a startup to help lead their business strategy around diversity, equity and inclusion.

All of these projects set my soul on fire. I'm not chasing money or taking on clients just to pay the bills anymore. And that's the secret to creating a six-figure blueprint that will sustain you. When you don't chase money and you do what authentically sets your soul on fire, you find that money comes to you.

Failure was hard; it was terrifying. But I wouldn't trade it for the world. What I learned from that experience are lessons that I'm able to use to help other people and rebuild as an entrepreneur. These lessons may not be fully learned in a book—you may have to go out, take risks, experience failure, and apply these lessons on your own in order to succeed. But let these lessons put you on a path toward creating your blueprint, taking the first steps on your journey, or making moves to live your happiest life possible.

The Lessons I Learned

One of the things I faced when I decided to jump back out into the world of entrepreneurship was a lot of doubt from family and friends. They too saw the struggles of failure and losing everything that I had and did not want to see me go through it again. I reassured them that entrepreneurship is simply a part of who I am. I applied key lessons from my previous business to Vision and Passion International—and I wanted to share them with you as you create the blueprint for your next business or stage of development.

Don't Be Afraid to Take Detours

When I decided to take a role as Vice President of Marketing, I told myself that I was only going to be an employee for 18 to 24 months before starting my next business. Five years later, I was finally ready to leave. When I'd lost everything, I had to rebuild from nothing, but I was very committed to the core values that I set for myself. Discovering those core values may take time.

Today, I tell entrepreneurs that sometimes you have to take a detour. Life happens. Whether you're running your own business or rebuilding your life in order to run your own business, you're no less of an entrepreneur. Know that every detour that you have is really giving you a lesson and giving you what you need to get you to the next level. You still can continue on your path to your dream of entrepreneurship and take a paycheck. But when life happens, you have to stop and do what you have to do to get back on that path that you know you were destined to be on.

This journey is not always linear, and it's not one that you're always going to walk alone.

Get a Mentor

I thought I was on top of the world when I grew my first business. When I saw my story in *Fortune* magazine, I didn't feel like I really needed help or advice from anyone. What I didn't realize was that my ego was taking over. And that ego was certainly checked at the door when I started a business for the second time.

If you're just starting out *or* you've hit your idea of success, find a mentor. Get a coach. I know you think you know it all, but you don't. Find someone that can help you create a network of people, connect you to clients, bring you to the next level and prepare properly. Don't let your ego rule your decisions. A coach helps you think about how your decisions will affect your business long term and guide you toward leaving the exact type of legacy you want to leave.

A coach or a mentor serves as another set of eyes. When you're so immersed in building your business, you won't have time to look around for your blind spots. And trust me—everyone has blind spots. You may not see the opportunities or deficits that are right in front of your face, and that's not a sign of weakness. Hiring a coach or a mentor who will help you see those blind spots is a sign of a strong entrepreneur.

Stick To Your Core Values

When you walk out of a room, what do you want people to say about you?

That's a question that only you can answer. A coach or a mentor can help you achieve it, but it's a question *you* have to be able to answer as an entrepreneur. Figuring out your core values is crucial to making the best decisions for your business and your life.

Opportunities will come your way that don't align with your core values. This was a constant reality when I owned my first business—but I took these opportunities because I was chasing money. I wasn't being true to myself, and it led me to be unhappy in my business long before I lost everything.

As I reflected on that time in my life, I promised myself I would not betray myself in that way ever again. I thought about what I really wanted to do, and that morphed into Vision and Passion International. Everything that I do now, from running my digital marketing firm to choosing clients to building my team, is done in a way that aligns with my core values and sets my soul on fire. And I couldn't be happier.

Discover, name, stick to, and reflect on your core values constantly. Take that time for contemplation. The whole "hustle and grind" mentality is cute for social media, but that's rarely how people want to live their whole lives. Make sure the hours you work and the people you spend your time with align with what makes sense for you.

Put Yourself First

These decisions aren't just partnerships, mergers, and deals. Make decisions about your schedule based on your core values and the person that you want to be. You need to sleep, rest, and rejuvenate yourself so you can be in the best shape to make decisions. Give yourself some grace, and don't be afraid to put yourself first.

Take care of your responsibilities at home and work, but also take the time to think about what makes sense for you. Our best breakthroughs come when we are relaxed. Take vacations. Take Fridays off if it makes sense for your schedule. Meditate, relax, and quiet the noise going through your mind. You'll find that a lot of times the answers that you have been searching for have been in front of you all along.

Celebrate Small Wins

Entrepreneurship is like a muscle. You have to break things to build them back up. Fail fast and fail quickly—it gives you the opportunity to take what you've learn and go on to the next challenge. With every goal that you hit, there's going to be another one that comes right after that. You just have to keep pushing and celebrating all the small wins along the way, whether that is a lesson you've learned or a smaller goal you've achieved.

When I look back at the losses I've suffered and the early days of VPI, I often wonder how I survived and got through the struggles. I got through because every day, I was just trying to make it to the next day. I was putting one foot in front of the other, keeping my sight on what I needed to do next and what I was put on this earth to do in my life. Each of those small steps got me to where I am today—each of those small steps were small wins.

Entrepreneurs have such big goals. We're visionaries, trying to build a world that doesn't exist. But if we're waiting until we hit that big goal, we're never going to celebrate and feel gratitude for what we've done so far. You have to celebrate the small things along the way to keep yourself motivated and on the path toward that big thing that you're reaching for. Celebrate small wins and success along the way, whether it's one deal or just putting one foot in front of the other.

Live Out Your Definition of Success

Years ago, I would measure success by how much my house costs, what kind of car I'm driving, or how much money I had in the bank. None of that matters. For me, today, success is happiness. Success is having time to spend with my children and the people that I love. Stressing about deals isn't success to me. I want to be able to be authentic and transparent about who I am, what I do, and how I can help people. I can only do that with a clear mind, putting myself first, and sticking to my core values.

You could have all the money in the world and be miserable. Who wants to live like that? If you're true to yourself, the money will follow you and it will be enough for you to keep succeeding, keep reaching small wins, and keep moving forward toward the larger goals that you have for you, your business, and the world.

Teaching these lessons to entrepreneurs and small business owners is what Vision and Passion International is all about—and when I get to wake up and do this every day, I feel my soul is on fire.

The Digital Blueprint
Derek Dlugosh-Ostap,
Executive Director of Pack Smart Inc.

In November 2020, I stepped away from my role as the president of Pack Smart Inc., the company that I initially founded in 1999. For 21 years, we have focused on developing advanced technologies that are used in either the digital print or packaging space. I still play a role in the day-to-day management of the company through my role as an Executive Director, but this change offers more room for the younger generation to grow, innovate, and move up the ladder at Pack Smart.

Throughout my career, I have noticed that not all of my colleagues feel the same hope and trust that I feel for the younger workforce. Many colleagues who are my age get frustrated with millennials. They complain that millennials aren't motivated or that they're lazy. I disagree. Not only do many colleagues my age misunderstand how to work with the younger workforce, but they are also failing to see the potential that working with these young people has for the future of their business.

At the end of the day, whether we like it or not, we are going to have to bridge the gap between our generations. Millennials and the younger generation are quickly becoming the workforce of the future. Failing to understand what these employees need and how to communicate the goals of your company is a big mistake. We can't just sit around and complain. If we want to start planning for the future, the older generations have to take the time to analyze how they are approaching the new wave of workers and where they need to change their behaviors, expectations, and forms of communication.

I see great benefits in hiring and bringing in a younger workforce. Instead of focusing on the way that things have always been done, we must look for new ways to approach problems and innovative solutions. Innovation has shaped my company, as well as the packaging industry, since its beginnings. We can't ignore the importance of writing a *new* six-figure blueprint instead of sticking with the blueprints of yesterday. Doing things the "old way" is like writing a blueprint on paper when millennials and innovators have moved to a more digital blueprint. We're past paper—it's time to pick up the stylus and start drawing something new.

Pack Smart, Think Ahead

Pack Smart's market niche, or core competency, is bringing print and packaging together. We have been bridging the gap between print and packaging since our beginnings. In order to innovate, bridges have to be built and gaps have to be closed.

Traditionally, printing and packaging were two different industries. Before founding Pack Smart, I worked in the packaging space with companies like Glaxo and Cadbury; these were my first career opportunities after graduation. But very quickly, I got bored. At the time, you could only learn so much about the packaging industry. To do something more exciting, I ended up taking on an opportunity in a smaller company that was supplying graphic arts equipment in the printing industry. This was at a very early stage of digital printing—we were supporting some exciting products from Scitex and Kodak, including industrial digital printers that were new to the market.

During my time in this position, I saw an opportunity. I saw a gap between the print and packaging spaces, and I felt that this gap was not warranted with the quickly evolving technologies available to us. Digital printing was becoming a much more stable product, and the quality of the digital print was becoming a lot closer to what we are used to today. I saw an opportunity in bridging that gap, so I started Pack Smart. Because of the digital print, direct mail and personalization started to gain popularity. Digitization of print really stimulates personalization, so in the early days of Pack Smart we started working with companies that focused on personalized direct-mail products.

Because we embraced the up-and-coming technology, we quickly built a reputation as the go-to business when you look for something unique in the direct mail. We started selling our systems globally. As technology evolved, so did our processes. Over two decades, we've deployed over 1,700 products worldwide, and we've participated in over 80 new product launches with major brands—companies like Procter & Gamble, Apple, Jio Reliance, etc. We've been fortunate to be attached to some of the most high-profile projects over the years. Working in printing and packaging isn't boring anymore.

We've been fortunate to build a brand and gain this reputation of a company that can innovate quickly and bring new technologies to market faster, reduce manufacturing errors, and reduce the headcount in the manufacturing space, specifically the packaging space. We were the company behind helping the manufacturing process of 15-minute COVID tests to be fully automated. Because of our modular design, we're able to automate or streamline those manufacturing processes a lot quicker than a traditional automation company and get products like the COVID tests out into the hands of the general public.

The solutions that we provide our customers is the result of the hiring choices that we make. We have never been afraid to embrace a more digital blueprint written by a diversity of minds. At Pack Smart, we hire talented people, we invest in people, and we hold ourselves accountable to our people, so they hold themselves accountable. That's what truly makes our business unique.

Investing in Millennials

I believe that being able to hire young people out of university is extremely rewarding. I don't see this younger generation as lazy. Pack Smart takes the time to invest in this generation, and the benefits from those investments more quickly than my colleagues might expect. When you see young people that came fresh out of college with no work experience contributing to your business, and they are 100 percent committed to your business, and they are doing things the way you want them to do, you feel validated and hopeful.

To me, it's more frustrating to hire someone who came from another company who has some kind of preconceived notions about what Pack Smart is and what we do. These workers are more likely to come to our team with a lot of bad habits. The younger generation hasn't had the time to develop these bad habits; they learn your way, and they value what they've learned. When they talk to their friends, they're proud of the way we do things at Pack Smart. I truly believe that this approach makes us unique and helps us stand out above our competitors.

In today's world, we are becoming more accustomed to constant change. This makes it more important than ever to hire people that you want to hire and work with people who you see making a positive contribution to your company. This process begins by making sure you understand who you are, who you need at your company, and what type of people you require to be successful as a business. And be candid with people. Before we invest in our workforce, we are very candid about what we expect and how we want them to grow with technology. Our team members appreciate that.

I want my team to take the time to understand what the younger workforce needs, knowing that we will get the same treatment in return. We want the younger generation to be successful in the terms that I have laid out with Pack Smart over the years. By understanding our definition of success, the younger workforce is more likely to help us achieve it. This can't happen until the veterans of the business clearly communicate these goals. We have to give our team members specific parameters in which they can draw this new digital blueprint that will bring Pack Smart forward.

Six-Figure Success

The parameters in which we draw our blueprint includes the three ways that we define success.

At Pack Smart, we first measure success by looking at customer retention. Our equipment is not cheap. The starting point from our technology is perhaps $50,000, and we build systems as big as $3-4 million per system. If we make a sale and we don't generate repeat business, we regard the relationship as a failure. Maybe we didn't qualify the customer correctly or we did something wrong in terms of supporting the account. Our blueprints have to bring us to a point where we are the go-to company for all of our customers.

Second, from a technology standpoint, we look at versatility and scalability. We aim to expand every product that we develop on a global scale. We want to be able to apply our technologies to different markets and different demographic regions. A product is successful when we can sell it in different areas. And because our systems are modulars, we are able to apply similar technologies to different market segments.

If we develop a technology for the healthcare industry, we look for ways that we can also apply it and sell it to big banks or in the retail space. Pack Smart is always looking, once again, to bridge gaps. We bridge the gap between generations in the workforce, we bridge the gap between different industries, and at our core, we have bridged the gap between packaging and printing.

Our third parameter is revenue. Revenue is important to a business. We aim for sustainable growth, and one of the methods in which we achieve that is through high employee retention. I think the ability to bring young talent has become very important to our business—our investments have largely paid off over the years.

We share these three parameters with our employees every day so they know what they need to accomplish. If they're not successful, they need to understand why and they need to be given the tools to help them become a success tomorrow. Throughout this process, they need to be sure that they have the support they need. This investment and respect for the younger workforce is key to running a successful business and seeing the blueprints that you have created come to life.

We've Made Progress

For the past two decades that I have run Pack Smart, I started my day with an unusual routine: I take a cold shower. This cold shower is a reminder of what life was like not so long ago. We have come so far in the past 50 years. Warm water isn't a luxury in many places; we can flip a switch or turn a knob and have warm water.

Fifty years ago, the technology that we developed at Pack Smart might have been considered impossible. The things that we do on a daily basis might have just been a fantasy. Our lives, and our way of thinking, has drastically changed over the past 50 or so years. We aren't done evolving. We aren't done innovating. In 50 years, we will make similar reflections about the innovation that will shape our world in the next five decades. We can't let old ways of thinking hold us back from embracing that innovation. If we want to see changes in our world like we have seen over the past 50 years, we have to invest in the younger workforce, adapt to their way of thinking, and embrace the digital blueprint.

The Lifecycle of a Business
Borzou Azabdaftari,
CEO of NickelBronx and The Falcon Lab

When you're the child of small business owners, you get it; you get how hard it is to run a business. You've watched businesses go through life cycles, and you understand that taking a vacation once every nine years is normal for entrepreneurs. My wife's father was a small business owner—so she understood when I scheduled our wedding for Thanksgiving weekend so I could pull myself away from work *for once*. My friends are children of small business owners, so they understood when I missed their birthdays because I was too damn busy. And I'm the son of a small business owner, so I understood the ins and outs of The Falcon Lab when I bought it in 2003.

At the time that I bought my father's company, we were doing just $200,000 a year in revenue. Now, we're making 20 times more. I know a thing or two about working with six, seven, and eight figures. I know you just have to go for it, take ownership of your business, and never give up, even when you want to throw in the towel. You'll want to throw in the towel; but if you are the child of a business owner or a business owner yourself, you get it.

The Lifecycle of a Business

The Falcon Lab started as a family business. My parents had a quick print shop—think Minuteman, but speedier. I was working in government contracting when my dad called me and said he's selling the business. "It's shitty work in a dying industry, but if you're interested, it's yours."

As I mentioned, the Falcon Lab was small when I bought it. They were doing $200,000 a year in revenue and watching everything transfer over to digital. Businesses just go through life cycles, and my dad had been coasting for so long without preparing for the parts of the cycle that were inevitably coming. He knew retirement was on the horizon, so he had taken his foot off the gas a few years prior. If he thought a potential client was going to be a pain in the ass, he would just quote them so high that they'd walk away. He was tired.

When he offered to sell me the business, I had to make a choice. I looked at basically my best-case scenario at the company where I was working. If I was going to be successful, in 20 years I'd be my boss's boss's boss's boss's boss's boss. And that path sounded way worse than picking up from where my dad left off. I left my job, worked alongside my dad for three years, tripled our revenue, and then I bought the business from him.

When I started working at Falcon Lab, I realized that small changes were going to take us really far. We didn't have high speed internet. We didn't have a website. I did a little bit of equipment and infrastructure upgrades so I wouldn't have to listen to a dial tone in order to check our email. My dad and I didn't always agree on the changes that I wanted to make (and he had to pay for,) but after a few rounds of making improvements that brought in more money, he had to admit that I was pretty good at running the business. Now, my dad ran a great business for a long time, but I was quick to identify pretty easy fixes and optimize that he had overlooked. I know I'll end up in the same position as my dad at one point in a few years, and I'll sell the business, too. I'll stop doing the business development that I did when I started and won't be hustling so often. But that's the story of running a business—there's a cycle that it will inevitably go through every 10 or 20 years.

My goal is to be able to make money in my sleep, but that's not always going to be possible. And that's okay. As long as you have the boldness to keep moving forward, everything will run through this circle, and you'll get to a place where you are making money in your sleep.

Just Go for It

I didn't have to start my business from scratch, but I know a lot of people who have. And there's no better advice for young entrepreneurs than to just *go for it*. People always have some kind of excuse to hold back. They start out by thinking they're too young or don't have enough experience, even though everyone wants to be around creative, young minds who have a fresh perspective and innovative ideas. Saying "I'm too young" is a terrible excuse, and it runs its course quickly. People who use the excuse of "I'm too young" use it and use it, over and over again, until their excuse turns into "I'm too old." Stop. Just go for it.

There's also the excuse of "I'm not smart enough" or "I don't have the right skills." But I think I've met a lot of really successful people that are not that smart. Unfortunately, a lot of intelligent people don't realize how capable they are, or they just overthink the downsides of starting a business. Intelligent people know that negative outcomes are the majority of the outcomes. Screw that. While they're overthinking themselves into a rut, a bolder person who isn't as intelligent is just *going for it*. Those people are the ones that end up being successful, because they took the risk and did more than the person who sat around making excuses. There's so much opportunity to succeed. If you wait until you're the best in your industry, you'll never start and you'll never succeed. Take the leap. See what happens.

The reality is, I think any business has seven-figure potential. One of my favorite sayings is, "I know a lot of guys who made a lot of money selling the sandwich that didn't invent the sandwich." You don't need something super novel to start a business. You don't need to offer a service that no one else can do. You just have to keep your nose down and you have to deliver. The difference between the Hair Cuttery and the barber shop on your corner is just that the guys at the Hair Cuttery had a plan for their business. They took the risk of opening another shop and growing their brand. They're not offering a better haircut than the barber down the street who hasn't thought about making a website. People get caught up on all the reasons that their business is not going to work, but then they don't grow, and they won't get to seven figures. Go for it—make your plan and just go for it.

If you have to, start your business as a side hustle so you can have some money on the side and you don't have to start from scratch. When I first started working at Falcon Lab, I worked almost nine years before I took my first vacation. That included nine years of working at least one all-nighter a week. But I did it, and it worked out. I even opened up a second business, NickleBronx, in April 2021. You can't let excuses get in the way. Even if that means *educating* yourself on the side, go for it. If you want to do digital marketing, learn about it on the weekends. If you're a consultant, find one person to be your first client in your spare time. If you want to do real estate, get your license and try to start selling evenings and weekends. The guys that started Warby Parker took forever to launch because they didn't want to quit their day jobs. But they stuck with it, and it worked out. It wasn't easy, but they did it.

I don't think most people will ever find a really easy way to make money. There aren't clever ways to make money. It's work. Don't get me wrong, the "four-hour workweek" sounds great. But not everyone is going to be able to make that happen. Tim Ferris was grinding for eight to 10 years before he found a way to put his life on autopilot. And even then, he had a really good product that he was able to sell online. If you want to start a business, it's going to take a lot of hard work. Don't let that be an excuse—you just have to go for it.

Moving Through the Lifecycle

Businesses have life cycles. Everything ebbs and flows. But at the end of the day, business owners need to be prepared and accept that they're going to hit these different stages. They need to take ownership when they get sluggish or they drop the ball. If an entrepreneur isn't able to push forward and grow their business, they need to take a look at what they can do to get to the next step and start making more money again. These aren't big changes.

Just hiring a coach is an excellent move for almost any business owner. A coach gives you guidance and holds you accountable. Joining an entrepreneur group will help you bounce ideas off of people who are in your same position. Or maybe the solution is just to hire people. I've been through this on both ends. Business owners are afraid to spend money on expensive talent, but no business owner's goal is to run their business 100% of the time. If you want to make money in your sleep, you have to spend money on people who are going to work through the night. If you're stuck and you don't know how to get to where you want to go, you either have to get a coach, or you have to hire someone who knows how to do what you need to do.

Don't think I haven't learned all these lessons the hard way. When the crash happened in '08, I made a lot of rookie business owner decisions. I paid all my vendors right away so they wouldn't be hurting. I let my customers take their time paying me. And guess who ended up losing money? Me. I had a lot of customers that went out of business before they paid me because I'd done business on a handshake and worried about *them* getting hurt. I didn't prioritize myself or the business, and we lost out.

But I owned it. Eventually I joined these three groups. I read a lot of business books. There's always a way out of a rut. The secret to success is not a secret. If you take ownership, take your time, and do your homework, you'll figure your way out of anything.

I think every entrepreneur wants to throw in the towel at some point. I did for a moment when we hit a rut, but I just knew I could figure it out. I just always believed I was going to be able to figure it out. There were definitely times where I made bad decisions and spent money on things I shouldn't have, and I haven't always been able to balance perfectly between spending enough to grow and remain competitive. This is all part of the lifecycle of a business. First, you go for it, knowing that challenges will arise. When you hit a challenge, you either have to figure it out or hire someone who will figure it out for you. Then you'll grow—until you hit the next challenge. And the cycle begins again.

Get Out of Your Business
Anant Kataria,
CEO and Cofounder of Sagacious IP

My business partner Tarun Kumar Bansal and I run a company called Sagacious IP. For over 10 years, we've been in the business of consulting with anyone who's innovating on all intellectual property matters. We work with big companies, Fortune 500 companies, and even startups, as well as anyone who's supporting them: patent attorneys, lawyers, venture capitalists and other private equity firms. We determine whether an invention can be patented, identify whether their patent can be sold, and find anyone using the patented technology so they may get some license and royalty revenues. There is a whole suite of solutions that comes with enabling innovators to bring out their products and technology into the world, and we support that.

Our business wasn't just built from a six-figure blueprint—it was built alongside customers who have changed what it means to think up, draw, and carry out a six-figure blueprint. We have both gained inspiration from our customers and our own experiences. So, when COVID-19 hit, we weren't learning things the hard way. We had developed practices and strategies that allowed us to quickly adapt and create solutions, even in unprecedented times.

How? We regularly get out. We get out of our business, seek objective opinions and define our goals with the help of advisors and leaders. We also get out of our routine, creating virtual crises that force us to innovate, strategize, and create solutions that come in handy when an actual crisis arises. If you want to build a six-figure blueprint, you've got to get out.

Get Out of Your Business

That's right. Get out of your business. Step outside of what you're doing so that you're not bringing every mistake, every crisis, or every decision back to yourself.

Tarun and I started Sagacious IP because we enjoyed working in intellectual property and we saw an opportunity to offer these services in India. All entrepreneurs start their businesses because an idea like this excites them; but we often fall into a trap of passionately following *every* idea that excites us within our business. Sometimes, entrepreneurs get very attached to their ideas and the way they believe that the idea should be executed. When left unchecked, in the entrepreneur's mind, the success of that idea becomes equal to the success of the entrepreneur.

This has happened to me in the past. I have been so excited by an idea that all of my efforts went to proving that my idea would work. I was stuck with pursuing the idea, even if all the data from the market proved that my idea was going to fail. My time would have been much better spent listening to customer feedback or what the market had to say and implementing that feedback into other ideas. If you're able to avoid learning this lesson the hard way, you will avoid many setbacks and spend your time much more efficiently.

Every now and again, you have to look at your business from an outside perspective. What would you be doing differently? How could you make your business more efficient? What resources would you need to succeed? Asking ourselves these questions is the easy part of running Sagacious IP or any other business. When we get to the point where we have to *implement* these solutions, our identity and our personal feelings often get in the way. Don't let this hold you back from making your business the best that it can be. Step back, get out, and look at your business like a third party would.

You can do this process on your own, but it helps to have an advisory board or a counsel helping you. These groups can actually look at your business from an objective perspective. Ask them how to run your business better and then actually *listen* to them and take their advice. The right advisory board has already drawn hundreds of blueprints and seen them come to life. They can identify what is going to work and what is going to cost you in the long run.

Give Business to Your Leaders

It's very difficult to get out of your business when every day you are managing every single detail. Of course, this is how all businesses begin. One or two people start the company and take on every element of the business for years until the company grows. Eventually, you need to hire a team. But don't just hire a team—create leaders within your company.

Every time Tarun and I have created a leadership position within Sagacious IP, we have been able to bring more stability or more growth into our business. Leaders aren't just employees—they take ownership over certain areas in the business and put more work into these areas than employees who see themselves as working on the bottom rungs. Having leaders also supports the process of getting out of your business. When the business is so closely associated with one person and one identity, you only get one perspective on the business. Our leaders have brought their own way of doing things to the company instead of following what me or Tarun were telling them to do.

Define Your Goals

These approaches—getting out of your business and giving your business to your leaders—only works when you have a rough sketch of your blueprint already completed. In order to find the right leaders for your business and look at your progress objectively, you need to have goals.

Taurn and I have always created goals for ourselves and Sagacious IP. Every year, we had certain targets. We never hit those targets, but that kept us growing more than we would have grown if we did not have those targets. If we just let things be the way they were, without any goals for big growth, we wouldn't have grown at all. After a while, we might have shrunk.

Your goals should appear unachievable to begin with. More than 90 percent of the time, you should look at a goal and feel like it's out of reach. When you do this, 50 percent of the time, your goal will not be met. That's okay. When you do create these "unreachable goals," you either end up having a reason to keep growing; or, in the best-case scenarios, you end up reaching the unreachable goals.

This advice comes full circle. Tarun and I have been fortunate to have advisors who have guided us to setting these goals. If you can't get out of your business, failing to reach those unreachable goals feels like a more personal failure than a necessary step in growing.

Get Out of Your Routine—Creating a Virtual Crisis

In the process of creating unreachable goals, you have to create unimaginable scenarios. I always advise business leaders to integrate a virtual crisis solution into your planning process. Crises happen. We all know this to be true. When you are defining your goals and sketching out your roughest blueprints, you have to think of a virtual crisis situation where things would dramatically need to change. Build a scenario with your leaders and then see how you would come out of that crisis. You will be forced to innovate and think differently about how you are handling your business and approaching solutions.

At Sagacious IP, crisis situations or adversities give us a kick. We enjoy the chance to start innovating—our passion for innovation and invention is what encouraged us to start Sagacious IP in the first place. In crises, we are able to see how we can step out of the box. Yes, this requires us to get out of our business. In times of crisis, leaders and employees are more likely to feel doubt or cling onto the ideas and identity that they associate with their business or job position. Crises force us to step away from those ideas and create something totally new.

When COVID hit, we saw the despair and the fear that took over many businesses throughout India. First and foremost, we wanted to make sure that all of our employees had high spirits. They needed to feel comfortable and that their jobs were not going to go anywhere and that they were showing up to a safe environment every day.

At least three weeks before official lockdowns were announced, we sent everyone to work from home. We also communicated to everyone that we were not going to fire anyone.

Once our leaders, employees, and board members were confident in their future with the company, we wanted to make sure that our customers knew that we were there to support them. We started to reach out to our existing customers more frequently, offering them a higher level of support without any extra cost.

Not all of our customers were negatively affected by COVID. In fact, many saw the pandemic as a call to action. Being in the IP research community, we go through scientific documents and literature every day in different domains—including pharmaceuticals. We knew that this was a time when everyone was working towards finding a cure, developing a vaccine, or looking for other solutions to help the world deal with this pandemic. On our end, we created a program called the COVID-19 Research Assistance Program.

The COVID-19 Research Assistance Program offered 1,500 hours of free research to anyone who was working on anything related to COVID: the vaccine, detection mechanisms, anything. If they were doing anything related to alleviating the stress of this pandemic, they could take hours out of the pool that we provided, free of charge. We assisted with the research, we gave them the report, and we connected them to the right people. This program was very well-received and well-covered by various government bodies. It was a great success.

This program was also a win-win. We implemented solutions like the COVID-19 Research Assistance Program early and found ourselves with extra time to get out of the business and work on the business. We were able to take a bird's-eye view of how things were doing and see the gaps in our strategies and goals. As we objectively looked at the results of the COVID-19 Research Assistance Program, we saw that we needed to spread the word about what we were doing *and* share the knowledge that our team had developed during this time. We started to create content and reach a larger audience. We created webinar programs, wrote articles, and published white papers. In a time when people were isolated at home, we used this content to build a community of close to 500 subscribers.

We would not have built out this solution had it not been for COVID-19. We would have not gained the attention and praise from government bodies had it not been for the solutions that we created in response to COVID-19. Before the crisis affected our business, we created virtual crises in our head. We got into the habit of getting out of our business and seeking solutions from a wide variety of sources, including mentors, advisors, and other leaders in the company. And we're not done yet. As we continue to practice these habits, we will continue to have six-figure blueprints on hand for whatever Sagacious IP faces next.

The Secret to Success is Consistency
Mike Ligon,
Co-Owner of The Ligon Group

My father was a land surveyor. Land surveyors are like most other construction workers—they work hard, get paid hourly, and are often driving around in a car with no AC and all of their tools loaded in the back.

When my father would come home from work, I would look through his truck, grabbing measuring tapes, theodolites, and transits. I had a habit of grabbing the measuring tape, going to my neighbors, and asking them if they'd like me to survey their yard. I didn't know the first thing about surveying, but I knew how to run a tape over the grass—and ask my neighbors to hand over 10 dollars for my hard work. As an entrepreneur in real estate today, I love to reflect on those memories. I'm certainly consistent (although I know much more about what I'm doing than I did when I first charged for surveying) and that's why I believe that I was able to succeed in business and bring my six-figure blueprints to life.

Years after I visited my neighbors with a measuring tape in my hand, I worked in land surveying and mapping. It's hard labor. You get out there every single day and work tirelessly in the field. My brother and I took this path because my father did it; I never thought that it would lead to making seven figures a year.

I never finished high school—instead, I spent that time surveying and mapping. People are often surprised when I tell them that. Recently, I was on a yacht with Grant Cardone, and after I told him my story, he told me, "You know, you're not supposed to be here. You're not playing by any of the rules. You're an anomaly." I *liked* hearing that. I liked hearing that despite my background, I didn't have limitations that other people place on themselves. I didn't go to college. I started working 9-5 at the age of 16 so I could help my parents pay my bills. People like that don't end up on a yacht with Grant Cardone, but I've never cared. I don't care about the piece of paper on your wall that tells the world that you learned something. If you want to learn something, you can do it without going to college. And you can make money from what you learn, but only if you can implement it.

That's the attitude that my family bestowed on me. Today, I work with my brother David running a company called the Ligon Group. We buy houses, have rentals, and do rehabs, fixes, and flips like you see on all the HGTV shows. More recently we pivoted and created Ligon Brothers, which is our brand that aims to teach people about real estate and how to find financial freedom. We didn't have financial freedom growing up; but since we were able to do it, we know anyone can do it.

We never once went to any type of realtor or real-estate school before we started our company. Once we started realizing what was necessary to be an investor, we realized we didn't need a certificate or a diploma to make six figures. Once, David was listening to a radio commercial for a real estate seminar. This was before we had started the business, and we were interested in learning how to start. But the seminar was $10,000, and we couldn't afford that at the time. Instead, we put our heads down, did our own research, and found out how we could enter the real estate investing world without having six figures to our names.

As we did our research on wholesaling and other methods that would make us money, we still worked full-time jobs. Real estate investing started as a way for David and me to make a couple thousand bucks here and there. But eventually, we took our real estate from making zero dollars to $130,000 in one month because we sat down and created this method that we call "link wholesaling." Once we implemented that method in our business, we experienced the biggest jump we ever had. The success of our method just blew our minds. So, we kept at it. We continued to improve upon our method and used it as a jumping off point for other facets of our business.

Today, we teach other people in the real estate world how to do what we did. I am literally able to show aspiring entrepreneurs a video blueprint to get them from zero dollars to six figures and beyond—the link wholesaling method will get you six (close to seven) figures. At Ligon Brothers, we also teach entrepreneurs other methods that can be used alongside link wholesaling or completely separately to bring them to seven figures and beyond. We never attended the real estate seminar, but now we run them.

Be Consistent

I tell my students that the secret to success is consistency. It really is, and it doesn't matter whether you want to get into real estate or not. I would tell any aspiring entrepreneur that—I don't care what they're doing. If you perform consistent actions to work toward success on a daily basis, you're going to achieve your goal.

If you're trying to lose weight, and you work out or eat healthier every single day, you're going to lose weight.

If you want to get a job in a certain field, and you network or learn something new or reach out to people every single day, you're going to get that job.

The consistency of the action is what's going to get you there. And consistency comes from focus.

If you can't focus on one thing, you're never going to be consistent and develop in a correct way that brings you closer to your goal. Focus on one thing, and then just perform consistent actions every day. This is true no matter where you are in life. I tell my students that if they have a nine-to-five job now, no matter what their age is, they're going to have a tough time transitioning out of that position. They have to ramp it up and start working six-to-ten. A nine-to-five pays your bills, but your six-to-ten builds your future. Whether you're in school or out of school, the same rule applies. Don't ever say you don't have the time—that's bull. You're playing video games, you're watching Netflix, you're doing something from six to ten. Work on your future. And if you do it consistently, you're going to get there.

Failures are going to happen. Setbacks are going to happen. You'll encounter obstacles and you'll have to restart everything. But don't let restarting or moving around obstacles hold you back from being consistent. Failure is inevitable in anything you do. You're going to hit roadblocks, you're going to have failures, and ultimately, how you overcome and respond to failures will determine whether you're going to see your blueprint through.

You could dig a swimming pool in your backyard with a spoon; it may take you 600 years, but you could do it because you took consistent action. I think anybody starting out in any industry anywhere, can set a goal and start working. Once they start, they just can't stop, and eventually they'll achieve their goal.

If you went to college, awesome; but that doesn't mean you need to do whatever you went to college for. If you have a passion for something else, do it. If you didn't finish high school, and you believe that you can't make six figures, you're wrong. You can. I've lived eight houses from the railroad tracks, and now I'm making six figures a month. I was just consistent.

Don't Do It for the Money

I tell people how much I've been able to make in a month only because it impresses them. In reality, I'm not a big fan of money. That might sound weird, but it's true. I hate the fact that somebody can go to work for 10 hours a day and do a harder job that I'm doing, hammering shingles on a roof in 90-degree weather, and make $10 an hour. I'm just fortunate enough that I had a mindset that forced me to look beyond the $10 an hour jobs that my family has worked and figure out the method to do what I do. After years of working six-to-ten and consistently working on my business, I'm able to sit back and have my company run itself. I make seven figures a year. I don't care for money as a whole, but I love financial freedom.

I didn't build this company with my brother for the money. I did it for financial security. I want to make sure that my family is secured in a way that I wasn't secured growing up. If something comes up, I have the money to make a difference and make things right. We live in a world where, if you really need to make a change, you need the funds to do it. I'm not saying it's right, but that's the world we live in. Fortunately, my business has reached a point where that is possible for me. So, I'm a big believer in pushing to be successful financially.

No matter what financial security looks like for you, you have to be willing to do whatever you have to do to achieve it. Sometimes, that means doing something that you may not want to do in the beginning to be able to do everything you want to do in the end. Nowadays, that's an unpopular statement, but I don't care. It worked for me—I reached the success that I wanted to reach by working those long days, being consistent, and always learning something new to help me move closer and closer to my idea of success.

Some people view success as being extremely happy at what they do. I'm one of those people. If you're waking up to the world, and you're living on coffee for fuel, and you just hate everything, you're not successful. I don't care if you've got $30 million; if you hate what you're doing day-to-day, you've done something wrong. You need to get back on track to a happier lifestyle. If you can wake up in the morning with a smile on your face, you're successful in my eyes. We all know that person who wakes up with a smile on their face. They exude happiness and they encourage everyone to follow their passion. People want to be around someone who is happy and successful; if you're not, you're going to deteriorate and drain the energy out of everyone around you.

I think success is just happiness, whatever that looks like to you. But you're only going to get there if you're consistently working toward a career in whatever makes you happy. So, take action today, tomorrow, and every day after that to do what makes you happy. Be consistent. As long as you're waking up with a smile on your face, you're doing something right.

Take Responsibility
Robin Sokoloff,
Founder and CEO of Town Stages

Each entrepreneur who starts a venture is full of so many different talents and ideas and strengths and weaknesses, and they should only sketch out a blueprint if they are using chalk. As you're running your company, as you're becoming a boss, and as you're taking responsibility for things you have never taken responsibility for before, a lot of what you thought about entrepreneurship will turn out to be not true. You will discover more about yourself, your team, your idea, and the market where you're trying to build your business. You have to be willing to keep wiping your blueprint and tracing your new way forward as you learn new things.

Let go of how you think running a business should be. Let go of what entrepreneurship is "supposed to be." A blueprint is fine to start you off, but just know that you'll be constantly redrawing as you go. Startups are challenging; they're exciting and invigorating, but they're frustrating. Expect to draw your blueprint once every 20 or 30 days.

I took the leap many years ago to becoming an entrepreneur. Today, I'm still learning lessons that I thought I could avoid in the early days of owning my business. I'm taking the blueprints I once had and erasing them completely. I'm learning how to take responsibility as a business owner, and how to take responsibility when things are outside of my control.

Taking the Leap

From the ages of 17 to 30, at any given time, I had four overlapping jobs in the arts space: casting, carpentry, dance, electric lighting; you name it, I've done it. But there came a time when I couldn't be helping someone else see out their vision.

There's only so much time and energy you can contribute to other people's dreams. If it's important to see that your dreams become a reality, you have to take the leap and go for it.

In my case, I had a dream of building a public assembly space that is affordable and accessible to all. New York City is a very particular place. It's the least affordable city in the country, and finding premium space for people to gather is exhausting and expensive. I built Town Stages in order to address rising real estate prices and inequities across the board in the labor market.

Originally, I didn't think that Town Stages had six-figure or greater potential. I was concerned with the numbers only as they pertained to expenses. Opening a 10,000-square-foot space in New York City requires paying hefty rents, overheads, and payroll. If making six figures was the requirement for keeping this place open and providing access to people throughout the city, I had to make six figures.

Of course, for someone in the arts, this can be terrifying. I used to make $11,000 a year as a dance choreographer. Going from that salary to running a space that generates $150,000 in overhead costs is no small feat. But I needed to believe I lived in a world where it was possible to have accessible spaces. I needed to believe I lived in a world that was moving *toward* equity for all people.

In order to live in that world, I had to take the leap and take full responsibility to build that world for myself and the people around me. Town Spaces allows me to be an example to other people, especially women, women of color, men of color, queer immigrants and anyone who has been held back from entrepreneurship, from free expression, and from different spaces within New York City. I wanted to show that it's possible to start a business and succeed with the mission of giving back; this kind of business needs to be more visible.

This is why entrepreneurs do what they do. They make the invisible visible. If they want to see something in the world, they bust their ass until everyone else sees it, too. With this drive, a lot of things that seem impossible end up possible.

Take Responsibility

When you're running a company, everything feels like your responsibility. Initially, it is your responsibility to get your business up and running. It's your responsibility to make sure that your team is getting paid and that your customers are satisfied. But as I've run my business, I've learned that there are things to take responsibility for under your own roof, but then there are circumstances that are above and beyond you.

As I've reached the six-figure mark and beyond, I've had to look at the things that I'm not a fan of doing or that I've been afraid of doing and take full ownership for learning and excelling at these things. The leap from starting out as an entrepreneur to running a super successful and sustainable business often involves not shying away from your biggest weaknesses and fears. In my case, I'm not a cold caller. I hate networking. Hard selling feels like selling my soul. But I know that all of these practices are the key to bringing Town Stages to the next level.

I always thought that "facing your fears" was a cheesy slogan that I needed to hear. Really, I just didn't know what it meant. When you build a small business, you often set out to do all the things you like to do. You sell the way you want to sell or manage in the way you prefer to manage. That's not going to cut it if you want to take your business to six, seven, eight, or nine figures.

Now that I've joined the Entrepreneurs Organization, which is a humongous international organization full of entrepreneurs whose revenues reach at least a million a year, I have to admit that my next steps include doing a lot of stuff I don't want to do. I can no longer ignore the advice of elders who've been whispering in my ears all my life.

When you're younger, people say a lot of things that you don't want to hear. You brush them off as pessimists, know-it-alls, or outdated perspectives. Now that I'm here, all of those things I didn't want to listen to and hear are coming back to haunt me. I'm finally understanding where this advice came from and why I have to apply it to my business now. There have been a lot of tough pills to swallow and tasks I've had to put back on my to-do list.

As I'm left facing the last tasks that I would want to take on as a business owner, I'm realizing the importance of tenacity, courage, and facing the fears that are getting in the way of what you know you need to do next. I'm realizing that I have to be courageous, and that courage comes in when it's time to step back, reassess, and make some big changes to your blueprint or your perspective.

Take Responsibility for Changing Your Ways

As a people-pleaser and a lady boss, I always thought I could run a business without being tough on people and micromanaging. I had to change my way of thinking. In recent months, I've felt compelled to armor up, suit up, and do some of those things that I didn't think I'd do in the future. But taking responsibility isn't all humble pie and putting your foot in your mouth. It can be a kind of game. It's fun to see the ways I'm starting to mature and understand the ins and outs of leadership in my business and in life.

Leadership often means being someone people are both very inspired by, very excited by, but also sometimes disappointed and frustrated with, and if not, resentful.

It's human nature to resent somebody sometimes when things aren't going precisely as you envision. It is unavoidable. So, I have to come out of this pandemic having dropped my people-pleasing way. Not all people can be pleased! Women are groomed to people-please, but if events have taught me anything in my business, it's that not everyone can be right at the same time. Admitting this took courage. Acting on it continues to take courage, but it's what I have to do in order to grow my business and be the best leader I can be.

You Can't Always Take Responsibility

I can take responsibility for what I wear to work today and whether or not I show up for night classes, but I can't take responsibility for everything. Nothing that I could have done would have prevented

COVID from coming to New York City and affecting so many businesses like mine. Of course, we all have to take responsibility for how long we let it last. And if I want to reopen my space and call everyone back to work, I do have to take responsibility for doing everything imaginable that I can to make that happen. Some things aren't up to me, but when these situations arise, I have a responsibility to respond, fight for my business, and look for solutions.

I also have a responsibility to revisit my blueprint and potentially erase everything. In the middle of COVID, I had to admit to myself that it was time to wipe down the board and start over. I have had to re-envision every aspect of my company and what the future may hold. COVID changed everything: finances, the marketplace, getting international business, getting tourist business. There are days when I don't even know if my business is possible, given the population in New York City and traveling and the combined overhead.

On top of that, I spent many years running a company while under a terrible administration. Everyone was going nuts and feeling unsafe for four years. I either knew we were going to come out of it or end up in the Tower of Babel. We came out of it, kicking and screaming, but we did it.

If Town Stages comes out on the other side of COVID, it will be another reminder that entrepreneurs do not have to take full responsibility for everything pertaining to their business. We have to simply respond, adapt, and keep moving forward.

Erase That Blueprint

Before COVID, I had to erase parts of my blueprint. During COVID, I scrapped everything. After COVID, whenever that will be, I will continue to face different challenges.

For people who like certainty and structure, entrepreneurship is probably not for you. For people who like to color outside the lines, who are brave and bold and don't mind falling on their face quite a bit and dusting it off and getting back up, entrepreneurship is for you.

Entrepreneurship, at this point in my life, speaks to me because I get to make that blueprint and then roadmap as I go. I can constantly change my blueprint or look at five different possible blueprints and see all the different pathways forward and get to play with that creatively. You don't always get to do that when you work somewhere. So as an entrepreneur, you know, if you like that freedom, and you don't mind the ups and downs, and you don't mind the humble pie you have to eat sometimes when you're definitely wrong—then entrepreneurship is for you.

Passion and Reinvention
Max Ryerson, CEO and Chief Digital Strategist of StratForce Group Ltd.

I started my company, the Stratforce Group, out of sheer annoyance. I've been an entrepreneur at heart for a long time; at 18, I started a website development company. My passion has always revolved around coding and the evolving technologies that were shaping my world. After starting the website development company, I started multiple businesses and enjoyed being a "serial entrepreneur," but around 2008, I went back to being an employee for five years. I was hired to advise a company on digital strategy, a space I've been comfortable with for decades.

I kept getting pushback. The company didn't hold the same mindset that I had developed through my background in coding. They didn't value the advice that they had hired me to give them. My employer held onto a mindset that many businesses hold onto as they slowly give up their potential for growth and change. I was so frustrated by the resistance I had been met with throughout my career that I decided to start my own company, pick my own clients, and let them decide whether they wanted to take my advice or not.

When you have a business, you need to constantly reinvent yourself. This applies to every industry, in every period of time. You can't always do what you do; very often, you eventually come to the realization that your strategy from one, five, or ten years ago is not necessarily sustainable from a market position. You need to be ready to change your business for the better if you want to reach six or seven figures. You need to be able to draw up new blueprints.

Are You Willing to Transform?

The first company I worked for as an employee was a publishing company. I effectively headed up digital for them at a time when "digital" was a dirty word in the industry. Journalists didn't want to blog; they didn't want to be "confused" with "bloggers." But the company needed to embrace the online space. I had to take journalists at the company through a recalibration of who they were and what their importance was in the digital space. Just because they wrote and physically published a piece *didn't* mean that people read it. And how would they know? A digital transformation would not only make a journalist's work more accessible to their audience, but it would also give journalists and their employers the *data* they needed to see who was reading their stories.

In addition to bringing digital publishing and data to the publisher, I also started to introduce digital technology to the events they were running. We had online schedules of the events, which didn't really exist back in 2010-2011 when I worked there.

Then I left publishing and went to work for a very large commercial real estate firm. I came in and put together a digital strategy that was market-leading at the time, but then I ran into a lot of issues trying to implement the strategy internally. The team had a mindset that the journalists had before they embraced the possibilities of a digital transformation. They didn't embrace technology. This wasn't uncommon for their industry. If you look at construction, you'll see that the way we build buildings hasn't changed in 80 years. It's not an industry that is quick to embrace technology. Realtors are more likely to embrace technology— there are some great platforms for people who are looking to either rent or buy, resell or lead. But even though the people selling homes have embraced technology, many people within the commercial real estate space are still hesitant. As a result, they're still far behind a lot of other industries.

The Jump Back to Entrepreneurship

Through this frustration, The Stratforce Group was born. The Stratforce Group is a consultancy that provides strategies for the digital age. There are a lot of businesses that refuse to reinvent themselves or embrace technology, but when I work with clients at Stratforce Group, I try to avoid or adjust that mindset. I'm also more careful about how I use the term "digital" now compared to five or ten years ago. For me, in 2021, there's no differentiation between normal life and the digital world. Through my wealth of experience and passion for technology, I've seen how the world around us has transformed. I understand the potential benefits embracing technology has for companies, and I'm not going to hold back from achieving this mission because some people who don't understand it don't want to listen. Holding back as an employee started to really affect every area of my life. I saw myself in a "sink or swim" scenario when I made the choice to jump in and start swimming. I had to work with the clients that I wanted to work with.

I had sworn never to go back to commercial real estate, but four months after I had started the Stratforce Group, the Blackstone Group came knocking on my door. They didn't need much help; they know their business really well inside now, and they have what is required to use technology to its fullest potential, but they needed somebody to come in and advise the companies they owned. Blackstone became my biggest client for the next five years, and I was able to run a business where I could enjoy my passions and build the blueprint I wanted to build for myself and my clients because I took the leap and became an entrepreneur.

Follow Your Passions

If you have a six-figure business idea, you've got to be really passionate about what you want to achieve. That's what will keep you going, because you've got to be able to change, take advice, be resilient, and stay flexible in regard to your goals. At the core of all of this lies the passion you have for your business and your vision.

My passion for technology and everything digital has been my key ingredient in the recipe for my success. If you have a passion to achieve something, you can exploit that. And that really becomes your foundation. I went from coding as a young child to building a business around coding. Then I used all of that experience to my web development business to form multiple other businesses where I was no longer coding, but I understood the digital nature of where things were moving in that space. I took the knowledge I had of the digital landscape and applied it to the publishing world, cinema, and my consultancy business. But throughout my entire career, it was my passion to implement technology to improve a current process that has always sort of fueled my next moves, my success, and the blueprint to everything I've done.

When you have a business of your own, it's very difficult to scale to six figures. It's a big job. But when you do what you really like, it's no longer a job. I don't work for my business. I enjoy growing my business, because I really love the clients I work with and what I do every day. I love seeing our clients succeed and I love building a team that shares similar passions about technology. Not every idea I have comes to life and not every day is filled with success, but every day I get to do something that I'm passionate about, and that makes all the difference.

Resilience and Reinvention

In the business world, a lot of people talk about resilience. When you have resilience backed by passion, you're destined to succeed. In every job I've worked, I've faced serious setbacks and challenges. I've needed to be resilient. In a past business, before I started The Stratforce Group, I went around the world meeting VCs, meeting product people, meeting potential partners, and getting a *lot* of feedback and rejections. A lot of entrepreneurs face this early on. Many find themselves questioning whether they're on the right path or if they've set the right goals. But if you're enjoying what you're doing and you're willing to put in the work to listen to feedback and adjust accordingly, you can't go wrong.

Listening to feedback is so important, whether you're a young and hungry entrepreneur or someone who has been running the same business for 10 or 20 years. You need to constantly reinvent yourself. As technology evolves, you grow your team, or you seek out advice from other perspectives, you will always uncover some value that you haven't yet realized that you can bring to your business.

I apply this mindset to my clients as well. Funnily enough, The Weather Channel used to be owned by Blackstone. Before Blackstone, The Weather Channel was effectively just a media company; but under Blackstone's ownership, they quickly realized that weather data was massively valuable for so many different industries. They had been sitting on so much data without realizing that they could commercialize it and exponentially grow their business. When they were willing to explore this potential, The Weather Channel ultimately transformed into a data company. This is the power of embracing the digital age, something that Blackstone had been willing to do.

Now, The Weather Channel sells data insurance companies. They've partnered with a big insurance company and created an app that would alert policyholders about hailstones or similar storms. Policyholders get the alert and are more likely to bring their car into the garage. Fewer windscreens are damaged, and less insurance paperwork is filed after a big storm. Win-win. That data has been available for a long time, but through the reinvention of The Weather Channel, this data is being harnessed in such a way that is so valuable for so many people. And that's just *one* example of how this reinvention has improved the business and the lives of its customers.

You have to be open to reinvention to ask the right questions, explore your passion, and potentially realize what additional value you might already have in your business. How do you actually build value from what you find? How do you uncover that value in the first place? How do you actually start to put in the effort to see how you can commercialize it for the benefit of your business? These questions require you to truly be passionate about the field that you're in—if you're not passionate, you're way less likely to ask these questions. When you ask these questions, you can reap the rewards that are transformed from the answers. When companies ask these questions and are open to changes, they can easily go from five figures to six figures to seven figures.

Creativity Under Constraints
Erin Fletter, CEO and Founder of Sticky Fingers Cooking

If there is one thing that the past year taught us, it's that creativity comes from constraints. There are a lot of constraints that entrepreneurs might feel as they try to break from the world of being an employee to the world of building your own business. But whatever your idea is, and whatever constraints are placed on you from the get-go, you have the ability to get creative. You can draw whatever you want on your blueprint, or scrap the idea of a blueprint altogether for something more creative. When you allow yourself to figure out how you are going to work within limits, you give yourself the freedom to find a solution in more creative ways.

Ten years ago, my company was under a lot of constraints. Sticky Fingers Cooking was an existing company that started out of a church basement. The previous owners were teaching children to cook; they worked hard and loved what they were doing, but they weren't running a viable business. I understood their passion, but I wanted something more. Quickly, I developed my own vision of what I thought that Sticky Fingers could be—a mobile cooking school for children. I was intrigued by this idea, and I believed it could make a difference around the country, and so I bought the business and became the CEO of Sticky Fingers Cooking. Since then, I've had to use a lot of creativity to work with a lot of constraints. I've had to redesign what a typical six-figure blueprint looks like and apply it to a children's cooking program. But creativity comes from constraints, and our creativity has allowed us to serve hundreds of schools and tens of thousands of kids.

Ninety-Seven Noes

I'm a huge proponent of after-school enrichment. I think it's underrated, and it's often taken for granted even by a generation who only had access to one or two after-school sports. In the next ten years, especially after the COVID-19 pandemic kept so many children inside, I believe that after-school enrichment will be recognized as the huge educational benefit for kids that it is.

In 2011, I thought of combining my passion for cooking with my appreciation for after-school enrichment to give children access to secondary educational opportunities through good nutrition. I went around to about a hundred schools in Denver to get this show on the road. Of course, I faced constraints. Not every school welcomed Sticky Fingers Cooking with open arms. I was told that I wouldn't be allowed to cook in schools, that children wouldn't be allowed to work in the school kitchens, and that our program was creating a safety hazard. Those were pretty big constraints—so we got creative. We created a mobile cooking kit that's perfectly safe and effective. Kids can cook everything from scratch, right then and right there, without needing access to a kitchen.

When we first approached 100 schools with our idea, 97 said no; they thought I was crazy. Three said yes. For some, this number feels like a constraint. I was just happy that someone took a chance on my idea. Our first client was a wonderful day camp in Denver called Dream Big Day Camp, and Sticky Fingers Cooking still works with them today.

Over time, those three schools in Denver really blossomed into about 300 schools in the Denver and Boulder area. We proved that our mobile cooking kit, and our process, worked. About seven years ago, we expanded into Chicago; today, we have about 200 or 300 schools in Chicago that we work with. Four years ago, we went to Austin, Texas to work with around 200 schools in the Central Texas region. Because we operated within our constraints and didn't take 97 noes for an answer, we have been able to teach kids how to cook with all the wonderful byproducts that come with cooking: math, science, geography, cultural awareness, nutrition, etc.

Growing Through Constraints

My partner and I took out $5,000 from our savings account to start the business. We're self-funded, and we've remained self-funded for ten years. We could have reached out to investors, but we just decided that this was the better path for our business and our family. That doesn't mean we had small dreams—I've never once wavered in thinking that Sticky Fingers could be a national cooking company for kids. Even when we've had very difficult times, that vision and my belief in the company has never wavered.

I know that this is true because I constantly checked in with myself as we grew, scaled, and even hit speedbumps. Despite any constraints we faced or how creative we had to get, I wanted to make sure that I was doing the job that I want to do within the company. Starting out in business, you are doing everything as an entrepreneur. When you grow and scale, you have to be self-aware and very honest with yourself. Are you the visionary, or are you happier when you are creating the spreadsheets and adding up all of the numbers? The answer doesn't affect your ability to be an entrepreneur—it just affects who you bring onto your team. A balanced team allows you to come up with more creative solutions. I'm what you call the offensive player, so I have surrounded myself with an absolutely incredible defense team to create all of the systems and workflows that we need to work with 55,000 children, to keep them safe, keep them happy, and to communicate with all the parents.

Eighteen months in, we also built a software system specifically for our business. The three schools were partnered with became 30 schools pretty quickly, and then 60. For eighteen months, we had been doing everything on Excel, and any small business owner knows that you can only keep everything on Excel for so long. I would be up at two in the morning reviewing spreadsheets, making sure nothing was incorrect—if something went wrong, kids could be negatively affected. To save me the long nights, we developed a software program and have been using it ever since.

Creative in COVID

There will always be a chance to be creative, try something new, and grow as an entrepreneur. A lack of growth can call for creativity—growth can call for creativity. Creativity is not limited to certain years, months, or seasons. Often, you don't choose *when* you have to be creative—creativity becomes a necessity. The amount of creativity that we had to pull out of ourselves during COVID was immense. Suddenly, the outlets where we could hold our business and connect with our students was taken away overnight. We had major constraints. We had to ask ourselves how we were going to make this work immediately, and we had to think outside the box for the answers.

Fortunately, my husband and I were able to keep *both* of our businesses going, if not thriving, during the pandemic. My husband has a fine dining restaurant. When COVID hit, he had to change everything so customers could order food to-go. The restaurant never allowed that before, and all of a sudden, they had to make this switch while ensuring that the food was still absolutely excellent. When our area started to open up to outdoor dining, my husband had to make sure they had the best outdoor dining that a fine dining restaurant establishment could possibly have.

For Sticky Fingers, I was able to immediately embed Zoom into our proprietary software; we needed to just figure it out and reformat all of our 800 recipes so it could be easily sent to children as they sat at home in front of a computer. Talk about constraints!

But that's business. In any business, if you just really take a look at what you're doing, a solution will appear that you might not have thought of before. Think of all of the new technologies and services that you used during the COVID-19 pandemic. These could have been created at *any* time in history, but because Zoom or Facebook or your favorite restaurant or your employer had constraints, these solutions appeared. Your business could be the next business to save the day when a pandemic hits, a business needs help, or any constraints are placed on a market.

Find Something That You Love and Get Creative

It's not easy to be creative all the time, especially when you're in a position or an industry that you're not passionate about. My gas tank or my reservoir of water never runs dry when it comes to cooking, kids, and creating new recipes; I am always confident that we can get creative and find solutions to any constraints or problems that we are facing.

The old adage of "find something that you love and never work a day in your life" isn't completely true—I work very hard, but my passion allows me to work that hard for the solutions and success that I want to earn from the six-figure blueprint I've built for this business. Find something you love, and you'll find energy to get up every single day. I'm not slowing down after ten years, and I'm excited about what we're doing and about what I'm doing.

I have this energy because I love seeing the smiles on kids' faces. To me, success is seeing the shock on a parent's face when their picky eater is talking about Ethiopian food at home. Success is having partnerships with public libraries, Boys & Girls Clubs, and YMCAs all over the country. We have a partnership with an alternative high school—the majority of the student population are experiencing homelessness. Sticky Fingers Cooking cooks there two or three times a week, and we have for years. Success is seeing those kids go through the program and end up going to culinary school, something they didn't know existed before meeting us. That's success, and although our idea of success is not the same as another business' idea of success, it still drives us to get up, find solutions, and get creative every day.

Ten years ago, I was hoping to follow a blueprint. I was looking for a six-figure blueprint that would show me exactly how to get from a small business in a Denver church basement to sharing my passion for cooking with children all across the country. But I didn't have one. I felt, as a native Coloradoan, that I was skiing off a cliff. There were no tracks in the powder to follow. I had no blueprint.

You don't have to have a blueprint either. Or your blueprint could be drawn up and feel limiting. That's okay. Even in the face of constraints, you have the ability to get creative. And when you get creative, you'll be able to find solutions and work toward your idea of success, at any time, in any industry.

NEW FLOORS, CEILINGS, AND EXPANSIONS

Lessons from 26 Years in Business Buddy Hobart, Founder and President at Solutions 21

When I started Solutions 21 in 1994, I didn't have six figures on the brain. My definition of success comes from my entrepreneurial mindset. I started Solutions 21 because I wanted to make an impact on other people. I didn't set out to make money. In fact, I started Solutions 21 at age 35, at a time in my life when I wasn't married, didn't have children, and could easily pick up and find another job if I was in the red for too long. Financial success would come later, I told myself. The company would achieve financial success only *after* helping and committing to our clients and *because* we were helping and committing to our clients. That's what really made us successful. That was my blueprint.

Very few folks have hung up their own shingle 26 years ago and are still around to tell the tale. Not only is Solutions 21 still in business, but we've also maintained our status as a seven-figure firm for many years. During the COVID-19 pandemic, we made the Inc 5000. This was part of our earlier goals, but they never came before helping others and making an impact. Our dedication to helping others helped us succeed. We hit seven figures early in our tenure and we've never looked back.

When you set goals, don't limit yourself. Have a focus, but allow yourself to dream big with what you can do as you maintain that focus. If you're starting a business, give yourself some room to be a bit adventurous, be a bit innovative, and to look to reinvent rather than replicate. The power of dreaming and the power of visioning is real.

So, how did we do it? How have we managed to keep the business growing for 26 years? We did two things: we reinvented rather than replicated, and we invested in our next generation of leaders. Our clients developed a similar mindset, and we're happy to say that all of them have made it through the COVID pandemic and outperformed their peers. I'm not asking you to replicate our blueprint directly, but by following our lead and developing leaders of your own, you're more likely to see your business still standing 26 years from now.

Reinvent, Don't Replicate

For 26 years, Solutions 21 has developed two major focuses in leadership development. We focus on senior leadership development and next-leader development. Business models have largely ignored succession planning and developing the next generation of leaders. They don't proactively invest in helping their team climb up the ladder. That's what we help businesses do—and it's worked.

I started the company originally because I had an expertise in a particular sales methodology that was needed in my former industry (office equipment technology). I knew that I could leverage that for a period of time, but I ultimately did make what would have been maybe a scary decision. I left my old industry behind because I didn't want to be branded as someone who only has expertise in office equipment technology industry. I didn't want to simply replicate what I had been doing as an employee. So, I literally stopped working with folks in the office equipment technology industry and began to work with completely different industries. Solutions 21 quickly became a business that is still pretty much "industry agnostic". We work across the board, from manufacturing and manufacturers in Europe, to professional service firms, to manufacturing here in the United States, to insurance companies. You name it, we probably have a client in that area.

It was also fairly common for consulting firms to chase the Fortune 500 companies, because they had the resources to afford consultants. But at Solutions 21, small- to medium-sized organizations are our sweet spot. We have a lot of Fortune 500 clients, but we recognized that we could carve out a space for ourselves in the industry by expanding who we serve. Small- to medium-size businesses don't always have the bandwidth to provide development for their future talent and their next level of leadership.

They don't have multimillion dollar training and development budgets or strategic planning budgets. We realized that we could be kind of a force multiplier for these smaller firms. We could take over that role and provide them with that same level, if not greater, of leadership development for their up and comers, than Fortune 500. And so that's what we did.

Again, this wasn't common at the time. When I realized that the mid-size firms weren't playing on equal ground because they didn't have the investment dollars that the big boys did, I realized that I could really make the impact I wanted to make *and* build a blueprint that no one in the industry was following. I did my research, but I didn't just replicate what other consultants were doing.

In any business, you *have* to not just do your research, but you also have to reinvent. Don't replicate. As I've worked with clients both developing their sales methodology and later their leadership development, I've learned that the companies that fail to stay afloat are simply researching and *replicating*. They look at what others have done and draw the exact same blueprint. If I had done this and stayed in the office equipment technology industry or only chased big money, I probably wouldn't have gotten very far in my business.

I know that the human tendency is to replicate and to be biased toward the blueprints, strategies, and processes that are already working. So, I have always tried to avoid it. As we expanded into different industries, I purposefully did not want to know certain things. I didn't want to be biased towards anything and simply replicate it. I wanted to run my business in a different way, and that helped us differentiate ourselves for 26 years.

Developing the New Generation of Leaders

Twenty-six years is a long time to be in business. I didn't always have the words to give advice like I'm doing in the books that I've written or the speeches that I've given. Part of the challenge of doing what we do, which is leadership development and working with other business leaders, is that if you're being sincere and you're being authentic, you also then have to challenge yourself to not be a hypocrite. So, when we are giving clients advice for them to succeed, we've had to take some time and look in the mirror.

When I've looked in the mirror, I've realized that the first 10 or 15 years as Solutions 21, I wasn't so committed to the team I was building as I should have been. Don't let yourself make this same realization 10 or 15 years into your business. If you want to make it through a pandemic, reach 26 years in business, or follow through in building what you've put on your six-figure blueprint, you have to train and support the next generation of leaders.

Early on, I was firmly of the mindset that leadership was about experience, leadership was about your title, and that leadership was about the time you've spent on the job. I was every bit as guilty of having that mindset as any of my baby boomer peers are currently. And this meant that at Solutions 21, I had some folks who were highly talented, but they were not necessarily folks who were trained or able to carry the business to the next level. I have since learned that we want to bring on talent that has a longer runway, has more emotional intelligence, and has more commitment to the team than commitment to their own individual results.

Teamwork, collaboration, communication and emotional intelligence is far more valuable to an organization than having the smartest person in the room who's only concerned about themselves. Many baby boomers still hold onto that mindset, and that's why they haven't invested in the younger generation. You can't build a business that will last for generations with that mindset.

At Solutions 21, we encourage business leaders young and old to make the shift and spend more time focusing on developing leaders within the company. If I were to look at my original blueprint for Solutions 21 again, I would make much more room to attract the best talent, reward the best talent, and develop the best talent proactively, from a leadership standpoint. To be honest, if I had done this 20 years ago, Solutions 21 would have probably been five to 10 times larger than we are now.

Develop and proactively invest in your next generation of talent as quickly as possible. There has always been a tendency to believe time was on your side and that leadership was a part of your title. If COVID has taught us anything, it's that one's title means nothing as it relates to leadership. Tenure means nothing as it relates to leadership. Work experience means nothing as it relates to leadership.

I have a brand-new employee, fresh out of college. I've been in business longer than she's been alive, but when it comes to a global pandemic, we have equal experience. Time does not equal leadership. Experience doesn't equal leadership. Leadership equals leadership. You have to proactively invest in my next generation of leadership as quickly and as aggressively as possible, and you have to give them the chance to make decisions, leverage their leadership, and motivate other employees. In these strange times, as a leader, you may not actually shake the hands of your team for months from now. You may not be physically present with those folks for months. So how do you lead them?

So many business leaders are kicking themselves, wishing they had invested more in their team and developed them more as leaders, but it's not too late to start. Leaders have to start thinking about what the workplace is going to look like in a post-COVID world. We're not going back to 1990—we're going to be firmly entrenched into the 2020s from here on out.

I'm proud and humbled to say that quite literally every client that we worked with in 2018 and 2019, in developing their next generation of leadership, have been outperforming their peer organizations substantially since the beginning of the COVID-19 pandemic. We've had one or two clients tell us that they probably would have had to lay off many employees, or worse, maybe shut down, if they had not made the decision to develop their next generation of leaders. Because of our training, when the pandemic hit, they had a force ready to deploy to hit some of the challenges that they were facing. Companies who failed to invest in their teams were stuck with only two or three senior leaders to answer all the questions and discover all of the solutions to the problems of this new era. Quite literally, every single client has doubled down with us during COVID. This is why we reached Inc 5000 status.

Solutions 21 has seen great success from committing to helping others, reinventing (rather than replicating) and by investing in the next generation of leaders (rather than relying on the old mindset about leadership and tenure). If we had learned these lessons earlier, we might have already reached Inc 500 status. So, take these tools, learn from us, and start drawing a seven-figure (or 26-year) blueprint of your own.

"Coopete" Within Your Micro Niche
Ralf Kaiser, CEO of Integrated Compliance Solutions and Greenlight Payments

Imagine running a business and not having access to banks. No direct deposit, no access to payment processing. Just think about it for a moment. Would you feel comfortable operating on an all-cash basis?

For cannabis retailers in 2014, there was no other choice. The Farm Bill would not be passed for another four years, so even CBD products were something that banks wouldn't touch. Dispensaries, both online and in-person, had to instruct their customers to an ATM in order to access cash, and that was just the beginning of the hoops that these businesses had to jump through.

Cody Hershey was driving through Las Vegas when he heard John Sullivan talking about these hoops. Hershey realized that cannabis retailers, however small of a niche they were in 2014, had a problem that needed solving. In a twist of fate, Sullivan was working at a bank that was located across the parking lot where Hershey and I were working at the time.

The two set up a meeting to discuss cannabis banking, and a partnership was born. Sullivan told Hershey that even though he had no idea how he was going to approach cannabis banking and would be willing to be a crash test dummy for anything that Hershey and I devised. This was the birth of Integrated Compliance Solutions, the longest-standing cannabis banking compliance firm. We are used by more financial institutions and cannabis-related businesses than any of our peers today.

Ironically enough, our six-figure blueprint wasn't built from a plan to tackle a huge industry and wipe out the biggest players. Our blueprint was built by finding a micro niche and cooperating with our competition—coopetition. Keeping these two ideas in mind, you can discover high-margin opportunities, easily generate cash flow, and be well on your way to six, seven, or eight figures.

Integrated Compliance Solutions

Cody Hershey and I promised to help John Sullivan, and we delivered. Integrated Compliance Solutions is a software as a service (SaaS) company that helps the financial institutions do the necessary regulatory tracking of cannabis-related business transactions. Banks have to know the normal operating standards and procedures of any of their cannabis clients; especially for dispensaries and other businesses that are heavy on transactions. We help them with everything they need through our software.

Our first client was First Green Bank out of Florida. Kenneth LaRoe, the CEO and Chairman of the bank, had a passion for cannabis and close, personal ties to using it for medicinal purposes. He was determined to help cannabis entities in Florida connect with strong and stable banking services.

LaRoe and First Green Bank truly opened our eyes to the potential that ICS had in this micro-niche of cannabis banking. Through our connection, cannabis-related businesses could set up a deposit account, pick up the cash, and bring it directly to the Federal Reserve. They were able to get payroll and insurance, which wasn't available without the help of traditional bank services. We were solving huge problems in a small industry—but that success was the encouragement we needed to keep going and truly explore the possibilities of this business.

Four years later, we encountered another catalyst for success. As we continued to grow as a SaaS business, we saw an opportunity in the payment processing world. In 2018, we acquired Green Light Payments out of California, applying all of our experience, knowledge, and technology to this vertical. Three years later, we are now the premier payment processor for hemp-derived CBD online merchants. We do payment processing with over 750 merchants.

Our meteoric growth started with small steps, but success leaves footprints. When you can focus on looking for those footprints and following them, you'll end up moving along the path to success with more ease.

Focus On Your Micro Niche

Entrepreneurs often start a business by focusing on operations, structures, and processes. Before you can do any of that, you have to find your niche.

At ICS, we took this strategy further. We found a micro niche, and it worked for us. In almost any industry or vertical, micro niches have the greatest margin capabilities and abilities. If you can find micro niches, you will find the businesses within those micro niches that have a specific problem waiting to be solved, like we did with John Sullivan and Kenneth LaRoe. If you can offer the solution to that problem, you'll find high-margin opportunities easily. If you've taken care of the margin, cash flow won't be a problem. On the startup side, cash flow can solve all problems. You'll be well on your way to quick growth and six (or more) figures just by focusing solely on micro niches.

If you are looking to start a business and draw up a six-figure blueprint, take that step back objectively, look at the market, and get very granular very quickly as to where the high margin opportunities can be found. In this research, you've got to reach out to businesses in those micro niches and discover what their specific and explicit needs. Don't assume you know what the needs are— have a conversation. Your focus should shift to really understanding the needs within this micro niche and creating a solution. That's where the margins will come from, and you will be well on your way to shifting your focus to growth or working in different verticals.

You never know when a micro niche will turn into a larger niche that you can grow into. The cannabis industry faced a certain set of challenges between the years of 2014 and 2018. When the Farm Bill of 2018 legalized CBD on a federal basis, we found that our niche changed for the better but still presented new challenges on a compliance basis for us to solve. Today, certain states don't allow CBD, leaving many businesses with questions and doubts as to what could be done and what couldn't be done. Finding the answers to these questions is what compliance is all about and that's what we do so very well. We look at these situations, we look at this high margin opportunity, and we put the compliance program into place.

Of course, looking at these opportunities has not been enough. We believe that success is 5% strategy and 95% execution. With excellent execution, the end result makes everyone happy. CBD merchants benefit greatly because they want stable and robust writing and processing. They want to know that when they wake up in the morning that they can conduct business. And applying our solutions and knowledge to this micro niche gave us a high-margin, high-payoff opportunities that have only grown over time.

Coopetition

There is another benefit to holding back and working within a micro niche. If you want your startup to enter a higher level—an industry level, or almost a niche level—you're going to find many, many more competitors in your way. These competitors aren't just taking a swing at the small problems you want to solve. These are true competitors with stronger foundations and greater infrastructure. While you are still a startup, your competitors will have resources to weather storms better.

If you really narrow down your focus and find those high margin opportunities, you'll find potential clients that you don't have to fight for with expensive marketing or discounted rates. By taking on these opportunities, you'll also gain the necessary cash flow for survival that would put you on the same page as businesses who might be trying to solve the same problems as you.

Competition has created an especially uphill battle for FinTech companies. FinTech companies have traditionally come on the scene in an attempt to compete with banks. We don't take that approach. Instead, we want to align with banks—they are our clients, and we bring them services and products that will help them grow their business and have a positive impact on their bottom lines. If you can do that as a startup, you're going to have a much easier time finding a place for your business—and other businesses will welcome you in instead of trying to push you out.

Focus on opportunities to not necessarily compete, but maybe even cooperate. You might have heard the proverbial term of "coopetition," or cooperating with what was perceived to be a former competitor. Use the same creativity and openness that you are using to find micro niches to center coopetition and but maybe create niches based on looking at some of your competitors. Are there opportunities to cooperate with them, in order to expand out a vertical, enter a new vertical, or even create opportunities for new clients?

We saw a meteoric growth between 2019 into 2020 by asking these questions. As we embraced coopetition, we took our revenue from six figures to 10 million at a really fast pace. Acquiring Green Light Payments and getting creative about our strategy as a payment processor really helped us succeed. We weren't going to compete with the big processors—we were going to partner with Visa, Mastercard, American Express, and Discover. If we had tried to compete, we would have crashed and burned.

As a result of this strategy, we've grown to love the payment processing side of our business. This is going to be the side of the business that we're going to continue to grow quite rapidly. We're also seeing opportunities in other verticals and other industries that have or are going to be putting CBD, and eventually THC, into their products as well. We're already seeing this now in the beauty and nutraceutical industries. Because we chose strategies that gave us room to expand, we are going to continue reaping those benefits for many years to come.

Last year, we continued our strategic initiative to grow by acquisition. We acquired Sterling Compliance out of Pittsburgh, a traditional bank compliance training and consulting firm that works with many financial institutions on a coast-to-coast basis. Ironically, for a business that started within a micro niche, there is so much room for us to continue expanding and growing.

Focusing on "coopeting" within a micro niche is what has made ICS extremely successful. There are micro niches and high-margin opportunities everywhere that you may have overlooked or failed to explore. Take a second look. With a clear focus and intentions, you will be able to partner, cooperate, expand, and build in ways that will have you drawing a six- seven- or eight-figure blueprint.

How to Solve Problems
Kumar Srivastava,
CTO at Hypersonix Inc.

In my career, I've helped businesses scale from seven figures to eight figures. I helped a company go from $5 million to $20 ARR in less than three years. I've developed a skill for identifying which businesses have the potential to scale and reach six, seven, or eight figures based on how the business' leaders draw their blueprints.

There isn't just one way to guarantee that your blueprint will create a six-figure business, but by implementing the strategies and mindset of businesses that scale, you will have a much better chance of putting together a six-figure blueprint.

It's Not about the Technology

Some of the most successful businesses in the past few years have been in the tech space, but the leaders of those companies know that their success is never about the technology. Any business that scales is created to solve a real problem. Before you can give your software developers direction, you have to have a very deep understanding of the problem space you are trying to attack. This takes a long time— you cannot read a bunch of blogs and have confidence that you can solve the problem. Blogs are secondhand information. Reading an article from *Harvard Business Review* is secondhand information.

You have to *live* a problem to understand (and then solve) a problem. Have you felt the pain of your customers? Can you empathize with them and speak their language when describing the problem? If the answer is no, you won't be ready to solve the problem and you won't be able to scale your business. Before you give any direction, you have to figure out a way to feel the pain of what you're trying to solve; otherwise, your solution will feel superficial.

This deep understanding will help you make the right choices regarding which clients you target, how you approach your clients, and what you expect from them in return. I think success, especially in the tech and machine learning spaces where I am right now, really depends on picking where you're going to operate and sticking with it. Once you've picked where you're going to operate, then you can optimize your company for that model. The companies that fail are trying to do too much and that rarely works out. If your product, at its maturity, is only good for the set of customers' prospects that don't have much invested in that space to solve that problem, for example, you possibly won't even get the door to be open to you. If you're constantly trying to build a project for each and every customer, rather than building a product that an existing customer base can integrate into what they use, you're going to work way harder than you need to. It can feel like a gamble, but you have to pick and choose where you are and where you're going. You have to pick the problem you're going to solve. This decision comes from a deep understanding of the problems you're trying to solve, and the level of investment in R&D and product that you have at your disposal. Not making that strategic choice or trying to do everything at once and create the perfect customized solution for each individual client, is essentially a recipe for running out of money.

It's About Working Hard

Understanding the ins and outs of the problem that you are trying to solve may be hard work—but in order to solve it and scale your solution, you're going to have to work harder than everyone else. I think people don't understand how much effort it takes to see a fraction of success that companies like Uber or Airbnb have. When you're a startup, you're competing with other startups that have been solving the same problem for a longer period of time. When you're a startup, you're competing with established companies that have the means to simply copy your processes and products as soon as they go live; you're competing with existing, large companies that can offer what you're offering for free as part of a set of products or a service that they sell. Startups are constantly fighting for revenue retention, and that takes *hard work*.

There are always tons of problems to solve. As you address small tasks and solve the smaller problems on your list, more will pop up. Over time, the problems that you have to solve next become more complex, larger and larger, more and more impactful. Solving all of these smaller problems gets you closer to the meat of the biggest problem that you set off to solve in the first place. And the way you do that is you have to work harder than everyone else to increase your frequency of problem-solving. You need a better website, you need a better sales team, or you need a better customer success function. Every day, you have to work hard to figure out what is not working right, and you solve it. The faster you can find solutions, the faster you can start solving the problems and exponentially increase the value of your business.

You can't simply hire your way out of this. The problem with hiring is that you get focused or defocused on the hiring process. When you bring on a huge team to solve smaller problems, you now have to manage this headcount that's growing in their careers and their needs. More people are not the answer. In the beginning, you have to just work harder than everyone else to solve your problems and to increase your problem-solving frequency.

Focus!

Hiring a large group of people is not going to guarantee that problems are solved. If your team is not able to create, communicate, or carry out the processes that you have built, you won't be able to increase the frequency in which you solve problems. In addition to solving problems and working hard, you have to create processes that will put certain parts, if not all processes, within your business on autopilot. As you face more problems to solve, you will face more distractions to try to avoid. These distractions will demand attention, time, effort, and investment. You are not just tasked with solving problems but also doing so in such a way that, if it's not core to your value proposition, you don't have to think about it as much as you were thinking about it earlier.

The way to put your company on autopilot is by investing in the right people, obviously, but also perfecting your process. You can't solve problems with band aids or short-term workarounds. Sometimes it's cheaper and faster to put a band-aid on a problem and get back to it later, but that doesn't guarantee the problem won't scale as you focus on other things. You have to have a framework to decide what you need to fix right away and what you can put off until later.

Hiring is a problem that cannot be solved with band-aids. If you can build the right structure and process around getting the right people, hiring becomes part of the DNA of the company and you don't have to think about it down the line. By focusing on the process, and not just the problem, you create an entire culture of successful hiring.

Problem-solving within your company is, at its core, a cultural issue. If you reward people who go out of their way to not just find the problems, but also fix the problems so they will never cause an issue again, you will increase the frequency in which you solve problems. This starts with culture, and it starts with you. If you build that culture, fewer problems bubble up, which means you're freed up to ask the bigger questions like, "How do I expand? How do I take my business from six figures to seven? To eight?"

Expanding with Understanding

When your mindset is focused on solving a problem, working hard, and creating processes that put problem-solving on autopilot, you are more likely to be successful as you expand and scale in your blueprint. Expanding a business is probably one of the hardest challenges that an entrepreneur has to face. You have to maintain a similar focus that got you to a point where you could expand. Your expansion has to be adjacent to what you were doing when you started your business. Going from one focus to something completely different is only going to create more problems for you.

If you want to expand, you have to start by looking for adjacencies where you can expand and where there is a demand. Fortunately, at this point you have a leg up compared to other startups or established companies that operate in that environment. But this leg is at a different level than where you started. Expansion is essentially creating a new company with a different business unit and its business model. If you're expanding to produce a different product or solve a different problem area than the previous one, everything has to be replicated and you may face a lot of the similar problems that you've faced before but in a new way. It's a big undertaking, and many business leaders underestimate that.

As you expand, what you're looking for is really a deep understanding of the changes you are making and the processes that you will be building. What is the risk? What are your strengths? What are your weaknesses? And then, how will you mitigate the risks that exist?

When I talk to business leaders about this subject, I always remind them of how this worked in the airline industry. So many "normal" airlines have tried to expand by creating a budget version of their airlines. The problem was, they tried to do budget airlines with the same crew, with the same ground staff, and with the same machinery. Essentially, the operating costs and business model were meant for charging much higher prices and having a tiered set of products in the airline industry, but they were selling it at a discount. Eventually all of these new budget airlines closed all of those business units because it just didn't make sense to keep them open. The airlines were using the same competencies and capabilities the company had, but just charging less for it.

In my experience, companies that want to expand already need to have some sort of a deep understand of how what they have fits into the bigger picture, whether it's the product itself or it's their reach into the market. And they have to use that understanding to determine whether, from an operational perspective, and from a competency perspective, at least 60-70% of what's required in the area where you're expanding can be replicated. If the problems and the consumers and the operations are too different, you're just going to be starting from scratch once again.

If all of this is done, you should have a high chance of achieving success.

To me, success is about how well you are able to convince your customer on the value that you're providing and what it's worth. It also comes down to getting your message down about the problems that you are solving, and having it resonate with whoever you are trying to target. The only way to achieve this is to follow the principles on which many successful companies have built their blueprints: solve problems, work hard, focus on your processes, and expand with understanding.

It's about Helping People
Kevin Connor,
Principal at Modern SBC

I've been with the same company since May 16, 1988. For the first 11 years, I worked as a sales rep. Then I bought the company.

After 11 years at the business, the owner came up to me and let me know he was ready to sell. He had a buyer set up and he wanted me to meet the new buyer before the deal was done. Now, I had just bought a house six weeks before. I was a little nervous, so I went out to meet the new buyer to make sure I'd be able to make my mortgage payments the next month.

I'm not the smartest guy in my field, but I knew enough to know that I could do just as good of a job as the guy who wanted to buy the company. My wife agreed. "Just make sure the bills are getting paid," she told me. I approached the owner of the business and asked him if he'd like to sell it to me instead. He replied by saying that if I could find two partners, the company would be ours. I roped in my sister and another sales rep at the company; on Friday we were employees, but by Monday we were the owners of Modern Strategic Branding and Communications. (If I had to do it all over again, I would not have used all those syllables. Today, we just go by Modern SBC).

In June of '99, three salespeople bought a company. We had absolutely no management experience whatsoever. We didn't consider ourselves entrepreneurs, but we considered ourselves desperate to stay afloat. To this day, I tell people that I'm a *despe-preneur*. But these three despe-preneurs (we became two when my sister and I bought our other partner out) made it work. We've managed to live a very independent lifestyle thanks to our business. We've kept the customers going. My sister and I can handle the sales and hire who we need to hire.

What's the secret to keeping a business afloat for 27 years? You just have to know how to help people. Part of that is being curious about what other people are going through and part of it is getting to a point where you can help more people each and every day. There's always someone who will need your help. In return, they can help you, whether that's by teaching you a lesson or giving you their business. But it's all about helping people—that's it.

I Know How to Help People

Helping people is what Modern SBC is all about. We're in branding communications; we're corporate storytellers. Our mission is to help people bring their ideas to life so they can market both on and offline. Whether it's getting the word out with a new website or getting other marketing materials made, I help our clients express who they are, what they do, and why they do it.

It sounds simple, but that's the mission I tried to stick by when we bought the company. I was never smart enough to look at the business in a very analytical way. When I think about my education in finance, I can say with confidence that I'm the worst finance major to come out of Temple University. But I was a despe-preneur; I wanted to pay my bills and feed a wife and three kids at home, so I stuck to my mission and made it work.

When I bought the company, I knew I had to stick to what I knew, and that was customer service. I love talking to people, working with people, and meeting new people. Above all, I love helping people. On the one hand, we help our clients with marketing and telling their story and promoting their business. On the other hand, we're always looking to connect with people who have a similar mission.

Modern SBC has acquired nine companies since I joined, and it's because we know how to help people. Marketing isn't very sexy, and neither are succession plans. I've met a lot of people in my field who have a successful business but don't have anyone to take it over. I come in and offer to buy their book of clients. We already know what we need to know about the industry, so the business owner doesn't have to worry about who's going to help their customers. On top of that, I pay the business owner, not based on what they've done in the past, but how they're going to help me in the future. They help me, I help them. It's simple. It's not a magic formula or a finished blueprint that you can apply to every business. I just know how to use my strengths to help as many people as I can.

Helping Myself Help People

There's no one blueprint that everyone can use to succeed because we're all on a different path. We've got different upbringings, different philosophies, and different skills. You have to use what you have.

My sister and I are lucky that our father was a car salesman. Every night, he'd sit all seven of his kids and his wife down for dinner and we'd talk about his customers. I didn't realize it at the time, but those conversations were all about customer service, attitude, and salesmanship. This is what I grew up with. These are the skills that I can use to help people.

You already know I'm the worst finance student to come out of Temple University, so you might not be surprised to hear that I wasn't in the National Honor Society, either. I didn't pass genius genes onto my kids. That doesn't matter. Every day, I tell them that they need to be able to walk into a room with people they don't know and be able to start conversations. They need to be easy to talk to—they need to network like I do.

I speak to a lot of high school and college kids—I tell them all the same thing, no matter who they are or where they're from. They've got to be curious if they're going to be able to connect with people. They have to be able to find something that they can ask questions about. I tell these kids, "When you're meeting someone, go from the top of their head down to the bottom of their shoes. Or start at their shoes—it doesn't matter. If you see someone with unique shoelaces, ask them where they got them. If the person's got a cool haircut, ask them what inspired the haircut." I'm telling them to use silly icebreakers, but these icebreakers open up the doors for a person to tell their story. And when you can hear someone's story, you can find a way to help them.

I keep a journal every day, and I write down all the stuff I learn from people and how I can use their stories to make me a better networker and leader and father. One of my mentors gave me one of the best words of encouragement I've ever heard: become better, stronger and wiser. I think about that every day when I'm writing in my journal. It's a philosophy that I've followed for the past 20 or 30 years and that's what I want to bring to my clients, too. I've become a better, stronger, and wiser person each and every year, and it's only allowed me to help more and more people.

Buy the Girl Scout Cookies

I don't learn all of these lessons when I'm running my company. Improving yourself and helping more people sometimes looks like reading a self-help book or reaching out to a mentor who's going to kick you into shape. Sometimes, it's just about buying some Girl Scout Cookies.

Back in 1992, before I bought Modern SBC, I was living in a small house with my wife. We had no money—my daughter had been born six months earlier and we were strapped for cash. One day in January, I get a knock on my door. It's freezing cold, but right at my door is this little eight-year-old girl. She's selling Girl Scout Cookies—they had eight flavors, they were $2 a box, and she was just selling the crap out of these cookies. I mean, going door-to-door in the snow is enough dedication, and she's got her whole speech planned out. But I was broke, I couldn't afford $2 a box. I told little Elizabeth that we were all stocked up on cookies—thanks and good luck.

I remember closing the door and immediately feeling like a piece of crap. I mean, I just lied to a Girl Scout, for God's sake. I never wanted to be the person that turned down someone selling Girl Scout Cookies. Next year, I'd be better. Next year, I'd have money in my pocket.

And I got better. My goal was to be the guy who all the Girl Scouts when it was time to sell cookies because they knew I'd buy cartons. I did it. I'd just give them all away—I could have eaten them all if I wanted to, but I gave them away. Every year after that, I looked forward to seeing the kids selling candy or Boy Scouts selling popcorn and just buying them out of everything they had. Once, I bought 40 boxes from a Girl Scout—it was all she had left. She told me, "Mister, you are really something." You can't buy those five words from a child whose day you just made. You can't buy that.

I'm not a saint. I just buy the Girl Scout Cookies and try to help more people every year. There's always going to be someone that needs your help, whether you're starting a business or giving advice to a new parent. How can you help more people today than you did yesterday? How can you help more people this year than you did last year?

It's That Simple

I'm curious, so I respect people who are also curious. My wife and I were in Siesta Key on St. Patty's Day, when we met a student at the University of Iowa. And he started asking me questions about my professional career and what he should do with his life.

I told him: Be adventurous, be curious, be willing to fall down, get back up, and stay in the game. When you find out what you want, go for it. Stay away from the things that you don't want and the people who aren't going to help you improve. It's not always going to be easy, but it's been simple enough advice to carry me through 21 years as a business owner.

No matter what this kid does, that mindset will help him. Whether he's trying to build a six-figure business or he wants to start a nonprofit or he wants to be the best father in the world, that advice is the key. Be adventurous, be curious, be willing to fall down, get back up, and stay in the game. It'll help you improve yourself, year after year; and most importantly, it'll help you help people.

Rising, Falling, and Pivoting as an Entrepreneur
Bria Evenson, Founder of Bria Evenson Fitness

2020, for many people, was the year of the pivot. A lot of people took a good, hard look at their habits and lifestyles and decided to dedicate more time to their health.

For my business, this meant dealing with a different kind of pivot—a pivot to thinking about the next steps for my business. I started building a new type of blueprint, one that included collaborations and connections with more entrepreneurs in the online space. I pivoted toward my network, building it and sharing it with people during this time when so many were fighting for their health.

This pivot comes years after finding my niche and space in the world of entrepreneurship, and then continuing to grow through a lot of hard work and building a team. I've put together many blueprints before this one, but I continue to grow and draw up new ones. If you are just starting out as an entrepreneur, know that your blueprint today might not be the same blueprint that you work off of in five or ten years, but that growth is how you reach six, seven, or eight figures.

What's Your Niche?

In the entrepreneurship world, it's so easy to look around at what everyone else is doing and hold back. It's so easy to hear what everyone is saying and lose your voice—especially when everything is online and accessible 24/7. But if you are starting a business, you have to know that you have a special voice and message that you need to get out into the world. Before I could consume everyone else in my network's content, I had to create and share my voice.

What did I create? I created Bria Evenson Fitness. I am a personal trainer and a holistic health coach who specializes in female hormones and helping women achieve weight loss and an energy gain after the age of 35.

What I do online is connect with other women who are struggling and help lower the stress in their bodies. We do this by cycle syncing, clean eating, and using other methodologies unique to my business and program. Clients can be coached one-on-one, in small groups, or in large groups.

I was able to build my business because I found a niche that worked for me. In a virtual landscape with a ton of noise, you need to be able to stand out. You need to have a unique point of view, a unique product, or a unique service, even if that means serving a smaller audience. (When you try to speak for everyone, you speak to no one). Entrepreneurs who work in the online space need to have a clear message that they can share day in and day out. Yes, this might feel repetitive, but it's only because we're so focused on our own message that we've drowned out all the noises around us. The only way that people will drown out other messages that pop up on their screens every second is by hearing a clear, consistent message *from* you that feels specific to *them*.

Developing Your Niche

When you know my story, you will understand my niche more. I have been a personal trainer for many years—but around about five years into building my business, I started realizing that my clients and I were going through big life changes together. My clients and I tend to be very similar: we're moms and we're in the same age bracket. What I also realized was that we were entering into perimenopause. Perimenopause is a transition into menopause, and this time in our lives comes with very specific symptoms.

My clients had a lot of the same concerns as me when I first started noticing these changes. They were overwhelmed, didn't have the energy that they used to have, and their cycles were off. The results they were getting years before weren't taking shape, even though they were doing the same amount of work (if not more).

About six months after I noticed this trend in my clients, I noticed it in myself. When I was told by doctors that I wasn't in menopause, I started to take a deeper dive into what perimenopause was and how it affected women who were trying to lose weight and stay fit. The fitness industry doesn't take perimenopause into consideration, so I had to experiment with different methodologies myself.

What I found not only helped me become a better entrepreneur, but it also helped me carve out my niche and *be* an entrepreneur in the online space. I like routine, and I like to schedule it. One of the most one of the most important things that I've learned (and now teach) is called "cycle-syncing." Women have a hormonal rhythm that actually allows us, throughout different weeks in our 28-day cycle, to accomplish more. Our energy rises and falls based on where we are in that cycle.

Our hormones dictate the feeling of being able to accomplish everything, so we take on a lot. And then there are weeks where we get very overwhelmed because of this same hormone cycle. Understanding this cycle gives you the knowledge to more properly plan, set goals, hustle, rest, and review. This is extremely powerful whether you're a female entrepreneur, mother, or just a woman trying to get through the month.

When you learn how to work in flow with your hormones, you can actually accomplish so much more than if you're trying to run at the same speed the entire time. Cycle syncing has been a secret weapon, but I didn't want it to be a secret for long.

I started to try out cycle-syncing as a way to work with my hormone cycle instead of disregarding it. Seeing those results were fantastic for me, and I shared my specific story with my email list and on social media. The moment I started doing that, I immediately got a lot of engagement and responses. My clients, potential clients, and people in my audience all had similar experiences, and were stuck with the same problems that I had before I tried out these methodologies. I realized my message had legs and that people needed to hear it. This was how I found my niche.

Feedback = Impact

Five years later, I get messages every day from women who are entering this stage of life and benefiting from the knowledge I've shared. They tell me that they had no idea what perimenopause was and how learning from me made a difference in the way they approach fitness and nutrition. Those are the messages, as an online entrepreneur, that you live for. They're the ones that propel you forward. They're the ones that keep you going, and the ones that keep you in search of more answers and more impact.

I knew that this business had six-figure potential when I started to hear this positive feedback in my messages from clients, whether they're just following me on my free platforms, or they've invested in working with me. This feedback is confirming that I have found my niche in the online space. Hearing the feedback about the difference I was making in people's lives also showed me that my business is making a real impact.

When I'm able to provide more value through more paid containers, I also get to see results in my clients' fitness journeys. Hearing about their results, their relief, and the joy they feel with more energy is really a big measuring stick for me. Of course, seeing my community grow, my followers grow, and the number of clients I have grow is a sign of success. But I'm not in this business just to make money—I want to make an impact on peoples' lives. When you make an impact, the money will follow. Through hearing this feedback from my community, I know that I am making that impact.

Entrepreneurship Is a High-Rise

Of course, this doesn't happen overnight. I always think of entrepreneurship like building a high rise: you spend a lot of time digging the foundation and a lot of time building the parking garage only to have outsiders think that nothing is getting done. To people who aren't working on the project day in and day out, construction looks like an overnight process. Building a business works the same way. People don't recognize your business until you have already put so much of your time, effort, and sacrifice into it. They don't see the blueprints you've created (or thrown out entirely). They don't see you digging, laying the groundwork and the foundation.

On the other side, skipping over the foundation may get you to high-rise status faster, but you'll be more likely to crumble. You have to dig deep before you can rise up. Not everybody understands this when they enter into entrepreneurship—I was fortunate enough to see firsthand, from my father, how much groundwork is laid before you really start building what other people see. That is what has kept me going in the early years, when it didn't appear (from the outside) that my business was rising to the top of my niche.

Expanding and Growing

Currently, I'm in a position where the groundwork has been laid and the building is visible to people in my life and potential clients. My focus has, of late, been about expanding my team. This pivot has its own considerations, but it is necessary when you're moving from a small business to a medium-size business and from a medium-size business to a larger business.

No one can build a high rise by themselves: construction works best when you have specialized roofers, electricians, plumbers, etc. It takes a team in life to be successful, no matter whether you're building a high-rise, building a business, or building a family. I couldn't have even done what I've done as a mother, partner, and entrepreneur without the support and ecosystem of my family. Entrepreneurs tend to be nervous about building a team around them, but I think we forget sometimes that most of us are already a part of a team.

Hiring is growing pain that I think everyone has to go through, but expanding into a team is really important to elevate. Entrepreneurship is designed to help you live your best life, not take over your life. If you're always a one-man band, then you're always going to be working in your business instead of on your business. Expanding your team is an inevitable piece of growth, if you want to have the freedom that entrepreneurship brings.

I envision that I will never stop growing. The blueprints I first drew up for my business came out of this idea that I could carve out my place in an online niche. I had drawn up certain ceilings, understood the groundwork I was laying, and started building. Now, I don't have to stop at the ceilings I originally planned. As an entrepreneur, it's so important to continue growing, pushing yourself, and bringing people along on the journey. Most importantly, you have to enjoy this process. Work within your interests, your body, and the journey that you want to take for yourself. Why would you build yourself a high-rise if you didn't want to live in it?

The Basics of Treating People Well
Janet Linly, President and
CEO of Linly Designs

In 2002, homeowners were really starting to take home renovation shows on HGTV seriously. They saw builders turn a home around in a week and became inspired to knock down every supporting wall they could find. But these shows don't always show the whole truth of renovation and interior design. No matter how big your crew is, seven days won't give your tile to cure or the job to *truly* be done right.

This created a dilemma—and an opportunity—for designers and renovators like me and my husband. We had already renovated a few homes as a hobby, but our guts were telling us that we had the potential to do more. I found a way to do what many interior designers and renovators on the market were failing to do: educate their clients. Interior designers in the area were picking paint colors and planning out a space successfully, but when they left the job, the clients didn't know much about the process or why something was done the way it was. I wanted to go above and beyond for my clients.

In 2002, I started a business making house calls, educating my clients along the way about the ins and outs of home renovation and design. As I worked, I discovered that there were a lot of furnishings and accessories that I could resource from other places, but I didn't have the space to put them if they weren't immediately needed to help a client. I saw another opportunity to expand the business. Linly Designs opened its first storefront, a 1,000-square-foot space, in 2007. If you stretched your hands out to your side, you'd hit the walls. Three years later, after the Great Recession was still looming over every business owner's every decision, we moved from a 1,000-square-foot space to a 10,000-square-foot space.

I did this because I knew that I had a six-figure blueprint to a successful business. Linly Designs was based on the idea that I wanted to treat people well, *including* my customers and my team. Even though that sounds like Business School 101, sometimes it's the basic lessons that build out the full blueprint.

Treating My Customers Well

We were so used to selling out our entire showroom that moving to a space ten times as large took some adjustment. Our immediate goal wasn't to dramatically increase our revenue. Instead, we focused on how we could accomplish the same look and feel that we had at our original space. Above all, we wanted to continue to provide the customer service that our customers had grown accustomed to enjoying. In the United States, we always repeat the mantra of "the customer is always right." At our larger showroom, I wanted to center the idea that "the customer is always right" in the sense of what they want to see and feel when they entered our space.

I am very fortunate that I entered an industry that I'm passionate about—I love working in interior design, choosing paints and patterns that will bring a room to life. But if that's all I was good at, interior design would still just be a hobby for me. There are two aspects to having an interior design business; you not only have to be a good decorator, but most importantly, you have to be business-savvy and understand how to treat people. You have to be a great leader. I think that going to school for business and having a background in skills like contract negotiation have been extremely instrumental to our success when it comes to finance *and* customer service.

Linly Designs is at the point that we can meet a client on Wednesday, and by the following week we're easily signing a quarter of a million-dollar contract. This is a big number—clients typically sit and think with that investment even if the price is something their family or company can easily afford. But my background in design and finance, as well as my desire to treat people well, helps me tremendously as I guide my client through the sales process. I make a point to thoroughly explain where their money is going, why they should trust us, and why they should feel comfortable signing this contract. I always tell my clients that if we meet and we like each other, it's like we're starting to date. When we sign a contract, we get married, and we need to make sure that at the end of the construction, we're still married. From the first home that I renovated to the most recent sale I made, I want to make sure that they know that we are here for them, whatever they need. That's why they put their names on the dotted line.

And we follow through with our promise, no matter who the customer is and how much money they have spent. We have a client who comes into our store twice a week after her yoga class because she says that's how she likes to decompress. She walks around the store, just talking to people. Our team knows her name when she comes in—we know every returning customer's name. We want to keep our clients. We want to continue to build the business. This is back to basics—it's better to keep a customer around than to seek out a new one. I believe this to be true, whether you define success by your revenue or just how you feel at the end of the day.

I measure my success by seeing our clients come back. Landing a quarter-million-dollar contract is no small feat, but when customers continuously come back after the contract has been fulfilled is a true indicator of our success. When customers drop in to see us and say "hello" or visit during the holidays, it doesn't matter whether we sold one candle to them or renovated 20 offices in their building. To me, success is not measured by how much money someone spends or even how many more times they come in a store to make a purchase. Success, to me, is measured by how they want to keep in touch.

Treating My Team Well

I love what I do, but I'm not driven by money. Money is simply a way to make a living—if we could pay our mortgages with jokes, we might all be living in a better world. That's not the world we're living in; but when someone is money motivated, I feel that they can only go so far in business. I get up every day because I want to see what change we can make. And I want to make sure that every day, we not only do our best, but we also strive for perfection.

This is a value that I share with my team and *for* my team. Instead of focusing on the numbers we hit each quarter, I am driven by the end result of how I impact my clients' lives *and* my staff's lives. I see how the lives of my employees and my team members and our vendors that we work with on a day-to-day basis have improved by being part of our company and I consider that a great success. I see the happiness when they buy their first house while working for us; I see when they buy their new car; I see when they when they just feel that they are moving up in their lives versus just working for a company. I want everyone that we interact with, again, whether it's a client or someone that is associated with our company, to see as much fulfillment in their lives as much as I see from seeing them succeed.

You have to want more in order to accomplish more. This goes for treating your customers well *and* your team well. It doesn't have to be about making money, either. You have to want to feel more personally fulfilled to be able to look back on your life and be proud of what you've done. Some people are okay with just doing okay. Not me, and not my team. I just want to make sure that everyone around me will want to get together when we get grey hair, relax, and reminisce on the great things that we all did together.

And we do it all together. We can already look back at the height of the COVID pandemic with a sigh of relief. When Linly Designs had to close our doors temporarily, I called my staff and I said, "We have to close to the public, but we have to keep the business going." So, we brainstormed ideas. We started selling products through Facebook posts and posting inspiration on our social media pages. We started talking to customers on Facebook, texting them and FaceTiming them. We wanted to treat our customers right and help them as they, stuck at home, decided to redecorate. For the four weeks that our store had to completely shut down to the public, we continued to sell our entire spring inventory. Then we did curbside pickup. Not only did this shift allow us to stay in business and treat our customers right, but our staff also felt like they were being considered, too. To this day, my team tells me that having a job kept them sane throughout the last year.

We could have easily shut down, furloughing our employees and twiddling our thumbs until the outside world changed. But we owed it to our team to do right by them and adapt to whatever changes must be made to our blueprint. Business owners should always do whatever is asked of them, and do it alongside their team. This isn't just advice that applies to your team; when you're negotiating with vendors or working directly with customers, you cannot ask of people something that you wouldn't do yourself. I don't want to ask someone to do something that I did not try first to do myself. When I worked at the store during the COVID pandemic, the first thing I will did was take a disinfecting wipe and disinfected every handle, every phone and every other object that needed to be disinfected. I couldn't ask someone to do all of this if I wasn't willing to do it for myself. Having high expectations for others is important. But having even higher expectations for yourself is even greater.

Treating Myself to My Passion

My background in business, as well as encouragement from friends, ultimately set me up to turn my interior design hobby into a business and a main source of income for myself. But it started as a hobby. I like to rip things out and then see them come back together. And I mean this in a literal sense; I don't just want to fluff up a couple pillows, put up a piece of art, paint a room, and call it a day. I want to make a difference. I want to make sure that the room is not only decorated, but it's giving my customers a different function and a purpose. Interior design is my passion.

And that's extremely important to remember as you start a business, run a business, build a team, and work with customers. No matter what talent you have, whether it's a talent for business or talent for design, you can only learn so much. You either have it and you're born with it, or you don't. No matter how good of a teacher you have, you need to have a passion for what you're doing. If it's not your passion, it's just not going to be ever enough.

Once you have discovered your passion, you need to treat people well. This isn't just basic business advice—it's the six-figure blueprint that has helped Linly Designs go from a renovation hobby to a thriving business that has lasted through recessions, pandemics, and any challenge that is thrown our way.

Risks, Opportunities, and Relationships
Brett Husak,
Partner at Flow Payments

T he first time I made six figures, I was right out of college; I got a sales position in the city because it boasted a great base with high commission. As you might imagine, very quickly I found out that I was good at sales.

But as time went on, I realized I wasn't just good at sales—I was falling in love with the industry itself. The more I fell in love, the more I realized I was on the wrong side of the business. Instead of being an employee, I wanted to be the entrepreneur. This realization isn't for everyone. Some people would love to have the comfort of a six-figure job, work for 20 years, build their 401(k), and retire. To me, that's not exciting. You only get one shot in life. I wanted to use that one shot to build a six-figure business and not just have a six-figure salary.

As I progressed in my career, I was able to start networking with owners of banks, owners of other processors, and entrepreneurs who helped me see what I could be doing if I ran my own business. Through building relationships with them, I was able to identify areas of opportunity for myself and go off on my own.

I knew that when I ventured out on my own, I more than likely would be successful, but I was still taking a risk. Entrepreneurship is a gamble. It's always a risk. When I quit my job, I was married with a newborn, which made the potential for loss even higher. But entrepreneurship is a cycle of *calculating risks, seizing opportunities, and building relationships*. Each time you move through this cycle, you can *set the bar higher* and achieve higher levels of success than you might have set out for yourself when you started. That's what I did when I sketched out the blueprint for my career; and every year since, I have climbed farther and farther up the ladder.

Calculating Risks

I understood the risk of starting Flow Payments because of my involvement in my existing company. I saw balance sheets monthly. I knew what the profits looked like. It didn't surprise me when, three months after I began my business, I was about $100,000 in debt. I've come back from that because I didn't quit. Don't let those risks hold you back from taking the opportunity to build a business. When you hit low points, you have to just continue to move forward. I made some mistakes—every entrepreneur will make mistakes. They will cost you upfront, but you'll also gain valuable lessons from those failures.

One big mistake that I made early on in my business was that I decided to buy leads from a company that was sharing them with other people. At the time, I didn't have every aspect of entrepreneurship nailed down. I only knew what I had experienced, and I didn't work on the lead generation side of my previous employers. I knew what the leads cost, and that's about it. I knew the closing percentage was, but I didn't understand, at that point, the value of the lead origination like I do now. I thought, at the time, that spending $10,000 a month to get leads would be worth it. It wasn't—the closing percentage was trash because we didn't know we had to be the first to reach the leads. I've learned from that one mistake—I know now to ask for a discounted rate on lead generation or to go with a different source. Sure, we lost five figures from taking this risk, but we gained knowledge that helped us succeed, convert more leads, and grow into a much larger company.

To this day, I still take calculated risks, but I've gained enough experience to be able to come up with that calculation and make appropriate decisions. That comes with experience and a whole lot of failure.

Failure teaches you more than success does—seek it out, and learn from it. And I'm not just talking about business but also life in general. I've learned a lot from failure: failed business relationships, failed business tactics, failed sales tactics. Don't fear failure;

obviously, try not to repeat it, but remember that even if you take an opportunity and you fail, you will gain something valuable that you can apply to the next opportunity that you get.

Seizing Opportunities

Remember, you have one shot in life. You should never be afraid of an opportunity, even though it might feel like a risk. I take advantage of every opportunity; I don't care what it is. Of course, I will calculate the risk on it, but I'll take advantage of it if the risk is worth the reward. You never know what may or may not come out of each opportunity that comes your way.

One opportunity that sticks out came from a bank that recently opened up its doors. It's a privately held bank for investors, and I put my money in it. A few friends joined me, but one of my other friends said, "I'm not going to invest. They're not planning on going public; I could invest in other medium-sized banks right now and have more of a dividend return or potential exit on my investment when they get gobbled up by a bigger institution."

That's his prerogative. But for me, personally, I've invested in this bank not just for the dividend but for opportunity. Investing is an opportunity to build a relationship with that bank. I don't know what will come out of this investment, but that bank might potentially bring an opportunity to me down the road, like a referral to another business that needs investment. I want to take advantage of every opportunity that could come my way.

I know that this is possible because it has worked for me before. My accountant brings opportunities to me to invest. Relationships that I've built with people down the road have brought me opportunity to invest. Opportunities bring opportunities. There's a lot of new industries coming out, and they're all opportunities to explore, invest, and build partnerships. I always tell entrepreneurs to take advantage of every opportunity they can—as long as they can afford it and have taken the time to calculate the risk of those opportunities.

Building Relationships

This isn't just advice for the new entrepreneur. Keep your opportunities open and take calculated risks, especially if you're already successful. If you've been around the block, you've already experienced what risks look like, and you have a sense of what it feels like to get some good returns and some losses. If you like the opportunity, take it. But don't think of it as just a revenue opportunity or capital gains opportunity. Think of it as a potential relationship opportunity.

When people go on *Shark Tank*, they're not just looking for Kevin O'Leary or Mark Cuban to invest in their business. Capital is a bonus. These entrepreneurs gain so much from accessing the relationships that Mark Cuban and Kevin O'Leary have with different organizations and different individuals that can help businesses grow. Look for those same relationships with companies and with the opportunities that are in front of you.

Your relationship is your capital in the business environment.

Setting the Bar Higher

Be prepared: what I've learned throughout my time as a CEO is that even when you hit what you would call great, high levels of success, it doesn't mean the work is easier or slower. If anything, success means that you get inundated with more opportunities that you have to calculate, assess, and take. I've had a lot more opportunities come across my plate in the last three to four years just by networking and building relationships. This means I can draw more expansive blueprints, but that doesn't mean I can put my feet up.

Fortunately, I'm not pining to put my feet up. I find happiness in the grind. To me, whatever makes you happy is where you're going to find lifelong success. I thrive on the grind, the constant working, calculating risks, and moving pieces around a puzzle. One day, that might change. One day, I might say that I've had enough and I'm going to retire wherever my wife wants us to live. I haven't gotten to that point yet, because I'm still happy with what I'm doing.

Some of my colleagues plan their retirement because that is what will make them happy, and as long as they're happy, I consider them successful. As long as my employees are happy in their current position and feel successful, I'm happy. We'll change them to a better-suited job position if they're not happy. But I'm not going to force them where they don't want to go. At the end of the day, you have to do whatever makes you happy.

Money doesn't buy happiness; it does buy you some comfort, but you have to do what makes you happy. I have learned through the experience of life, even though I'm 37, I will probably never fully retire because working makes me happy. I'm not everyone, but I have my idea of what will make me happy.

You have to know what makes you happy in order to set your goals. You have to set your goals in order to reach your idea of success. If you're trying to set the bar higher for yourself and reach success, but you don't have goals, you might as well be on a ship in a sea without a compass.

Your end result may be that you want to build an eight-figure or nine-figure company that you can exit in 5, 10, or 20 years. The exact numbers don't matter as long as they make you happy and they're realistic. Being realistic means that your end goals might change. My end goal has changed since I started Flow Payments because I've already hit my goal. You may change your goal for another reason—that's okay. I have a personal friend who exited an eight, high eight-figure exit. Originally, he told me that during his next exit, he was going for nine. But he changed that; later he told me that he wasn't going to hit nine, so he was going to strive for eight. That's not a bad goal to hit, even if it's lower than the goal that was originally set. Your goals will change as you kind of go through the ups and downs of entrepreneurship, but as long as you're happy, I believe you are successful.

Defining your goals and your idea of success is just like any other part of being an entrepreneur. They are an opportunity to push forward or reflect. Setting goals comes with a risk of not achieving them or not hitting your maximum potential. Calculate those risks, but don't be afraid to seize that opportunity. At the end of the day, you might fail and learned something new, but that's the journey of being an entrepreneur. And what a great journey it is.

Nonprofit or For-profit, Draw Your Blueprint with Your Team
Korrie Mae Wiszniak, CEO of Kids@ Churchill Park

My colleagues may be surprised to see my name in a book about six-figure blueprints. As a reader, you might be surprised to learn that I run a non-profit. But even though the organization I run is a nonprofit, I still know a thing or two about growing a business and leading your team to six or seven figures.

Before I became the Chief Executive Officer of Kids@ Churchill Park, I ran companies in and outside of the education space. I was the CEO of a Montessori preschool and co-founded a boutique custom home-building organization. I had over 20 years of experience creating strategies and seeing out the vision that I had for my businesses.

I had never been with a nonprofit before, but I was contacted by a headhunter on LinkedIn who appreciated my business background and asked if I was interested. Running a nonprofit was on my bucket list, so I thought I would give it a shot. A few months later, I had the position. Taking this chance has been one of the best moves I've made; not only for my career, but also for the opportunity to touch people, move the organization forward, and watch children grow and learn.

The Six-Figure Blueprint for Nonprofits

The first thing I did when I first started with Kids@ Churchill Park was to sit the team down for a strategic planning session. Together, we revisited our vision, our mission, and our values. We asked ourselves questions that any organization, whether it's a nonprofit, a startup, or any other business, would ask themselves. Where do we want to be? Where do we see ourselves? What does success look like for us?

There are more similarities between nonprofits and for-profit businesses than some people might realize. Unfortunately, non-profit CEOs, (or executive directors, as they're normally called) tend to be pressured to separate the two. That's not what I do, and that's why I was hired. A non-profit is still a business; it's a business that provides for people without getting something substantial back. Obviously, everyone receives a paycheck, but at the same time, it's really nice to be able to say to your customers that we're working together because we're really passionate about what we do.

Rather than focusing on a six-figure profit, non-profits just see success differently. We ask ourselves: How do we reach more people? How do we serve more families? How do we ignite more children's potential? How do we nurture more curious minds, happy hearts, and healthy bodies? The answer is similar to any other business that wants to make a profit. We obviously have to expand. So, when I started at Kids@ Churchill Park, I wasn't afraid to ask these questions and look at the organization like any other business. I wanted to scale the services that we provide families. I wanted to build more centers, offer more programs, and put more money back into the business. I wanted to draw up a blueprint just like I would for any other business—and that's exactly what I did.

Setting Goals

Whether you run a nonprofit or a startup, you can reach your "six figures" by setting goals. KPIs and goals are important—but it's *really* important to continue to revisit those goals. And what's *most* important is that everyone on your team comes together to communicate and understand those goals.

The goals I set for Kids@ Churchill Park are big. The goals I set for all of my businesses are big. I believe that you have to make your goals big and dream big. You can achieve those goals if you plan consistently, communicate regularly, and revisit your goals periodically.

Of course, your goals might change. When COVID came along, our goals changed. Originally, our goal was to get as many families as we could enrolled in full-time programs. That goal no longer made sense when COVID hit. Our overarching goal has always been to have our programs be a second home for kids. We wanted our families to view us as their second family. How do we do that if we're not offering drop-in care, or we're not offering part-time care, when that's what our families need?

We needed to focus more of our attention on offering part-time programs, drop-in services, and other things that our families really needed to get through the pandemic. That's a change we didn't anticipate before COVID, but one that we had to make when we revisited our goals.

As a leader, you have to be really agile, always having curiosity and really being persistent in driving toward your goals, but then not being afraid to pivot when there's a shift and the path you're on is no longer serving your larger mission. Or maybe you decide to pivot because you realize that your previous ideas weren't so great. As a leader, I'm going to come up with some great ideas and I'm going to come up with some crappy ideas. Every leader or entrepreneur is going to come up with great ideas and some crappy ideas. But I'm confident that as long as my team is focused on the families that we serve and the children that we serve, those ideas will sort themselves out.

You're not always going to be on the right path. You're not always going to make the right choices. Don't let that intimidate you into setting small goals, because part of setting big goals is striving to fail.

If you're striving to fail, it means you're going to win, eventually. Everything will sort itself out when you have the right team supporting you and choosing to learn from failure. I believe that if you haven't experienced failure, then you're really not pushing and you're not dreaming big enough. If you haven't failed, you're probably staying in a safe zone. Who wants to stay in the safe zone forever?

Being Transparent for Your Team

Often, people don't dream big enough because it's scary. Regardless of the success that business owners have had, there is often still a lingering fear of failing or making mistakes. People don't want to admit their mistakes.

I'm not like most people.

During COVID, I really wanted to make sure that my team was communicating even more, even in the face of mistakes or uncertainty. We knew less about our plans than we ever had, but that didn't mean that we had to hold back from communicating with each other and our families. I'm not afraid to tell my team that I've made a mistake or tell families that we need to change our plans and policies due to new information that came to light regarding the COVID pandemic. I'm not afraid to be transparent.

I know people who loosely toss the word "transparency" around. But it truly is important to communication, morale, customer retention, and every facet of your organization. Sometimes, "transparency" just means communicating the things people *want* to know, rather than prioritizing the things that we *want* them to know. There are always going to be things that you don't know or that you are working through—transparency is about communicating those things and thanking your team, your customers, or the general public for their patience. We didn't always know what our organization was going to look like during the pandemic, but we promised everyone that we were going to work through it together. I vowed to keep my team in the loop and ask for feedback as things changed. We communicated that no matter how the world situation changes, we are staying steadfast to our mission, which is to provide your children with the best care possible. Even when you don't have all the answers, transparency and reassurance is comforting.

I didn't want my team or my families to sit at home wondering if we were going to close centers or if team members were going to lose their jobs over the pandemic. We were fortunate to be able to open a new center, but we were transparent throughout the entire process. We weren't sure if anyone could come to the center when it opened because everything was closed down, but this was communicated as we planned to open. We let our team know that we weren't sure if we're going to get kids at this one center, but we reassured them that we had a plan for the next couple of years and were doing fine. This reassurance allowed our team to confidently do their jobs and our families to stick with us.

Unfortunately, in business, sometimes you do have to let people go. During the pandemic, we did have to let people go, but throughout the process we were transparent. We communicated how goals were met and that meant certain positions weren't required. We also communicated that there were other positions available and what our plans were for keeping team members employed even as our goals changed. Even when the message was hard to send, we were committed to being transparent.

Living Our Values

Transparency is a part of our six-figure blueprint. Our values make up the structure of our organization. And in order to see our plans come to life, I've got to live our values.

As a CEO, you are the least important person in your organization. It's true. There's no room for a CEO who doesn't think they have a lot to learn. There's no room for a CEO who doesn't live out the values of the company. For me, living out our values means that I love the people involved at Kids@ Churchill Park. Living out our values means that I put people first.

If you really understand people and you empathize with them, you will have a much easier time bringing people along with you on your journey. When you're transparent with people, they are more likely to join you, too. People want to know where they are going. They want to believe that the person they are following is confident, tenacious, and has the team's best interests in mind. That's what you have to do as a leader. You're not leading people who don't necessarily want to follow—you're all going on a journey together. That's the only way you'll get to where you want to go.

The route may be different, and the path may be different from the one that you originally set out on. But when we have to change our route, the entire team knows where we are going. We keep our eye on the prize because that's where we all agreed we want to be. For some teams, that's a six- or seven-figure business. For others, that's an organization that serves families across the country. Regardless, the team moves as one, together. We learn from failure, celebrate our success, and communicate along the way.

Aim For Infinity
Amber Howard, Founder and CEO of
Amber Howard and Associates

For many people, making six figures is a goal. For others, it's an impossibility. At the age of 16, when I dropped out of school to have my first child, making six figures wasn't on my mind. I was starting a family. I had a second child the next year and got married at 18. It wasn't until I reached my 20s that I put myself through university, got my degree, and formally started my career.

Today, my life looks different. My children are 25, 24, and 14 now. I recently made the shift away from my corporate career to start Amber Howard and Associates. And of course, the world has changed dramatically in the last *two* years, much less the last 25 years. But throughout it all, I persevered. My blueprint in life didn't always have exact measurements—to this day, I believe that people have largely limited themselves to society's different measures for what success and happiness are supposed to look like. But by persevering through all of my life's challenges, I was able to build a life and a career that has helped me achieve *my* definition of success.

I have always known that I was born to make a difference in people's lives. My story is one of always seeking out the difference that I can make for people and how I can help them truly love the journey that they are taking. Even outside of my career, my story is a love story. It's a story of love from my mom and my father, and how they persevered in order to create me and live their lives. My story is a love story of my children—of getting married young, being a teen mom, and starting a career later than my peers. I've had to persevere and harness all of the grit in me, because I was really driven to provide a good life for my kids. My story is also a story of falling in love with myself, and really coming and doing the work. I'm still on this journey. You're still on this journey. And your journey has the potential to aim for infinity.

This is the blueprint that I share with my small- to medium-business clients that I work with at Amber Howard and Associates. Notice that I don't focus specifically on six figures. I believe that our vision and goals for ourselves should be *infinite,* and that we should persevere indefinitely. We should not be stopped because we have limited resources. We should not be stopped by "failures". And most importantly, we should not be stopped by limiting beliefs. This continuous perseverance is at the heart of my story, and the heart of many stories from entrepreneurs who found a way to aim for infinity.

Money Is a Form of Infinite Energy

Amber Howard and Associates opened in September of last year. We offer consulting, coaching, training, and development for small- to medium-sized businesses. I didn't just open my business because it has six-figure potential; I'm really looking to fill in some gaps that we see in the industry. Larger companies that work with larger clients leave many small businesses behind. My company aims to provide accessible services to individuals and people who may not have access to management consultants or specialized training programs that are just for them.

Throughout my career, I have worked with a lot of small business owners who open their business because they're really passionate about a product, good, or a service that they have to offer, but they don't necessarily have the training in how to operate a business with integrity or how to truly optimize the product, good, or service that they're providing. There are so many opportunities to help these small business owners pair the passion they have with the resources, awareness, and knowledge they truly need to succeed.

Money, whether a business has a lot or a little of it, is just a form of energy. We're always exchanging services for money or for goods. We're exchanging a commitment to our clients for the energy that they give back, whether it's a monetary form of energy or otherwise.

Money is one of the limits that often holds people back as they develop their business: they don't know how to gauge how much money to ask for, they don't know how they're going to have enough money to reach certain goals, or they want to hold onto the money they do have instead of investing it in their products or people. But we can't create blueprints with these limits. When I encounter business owners worried about money or other limiting beliefs, I tell them they have to let go and go for what they want. As business owners, we have to give up trying to figure out the *how*, because the *how* is really none of our business. The *how* sorts itself out as we move toward our dreams, just like the resources that you need. Money and resources will show up on that journey as long as we believe in ourselves and are passionate about what it is that we're creating.

Set Infinite Goals

This type of mindset can be scary for many people who have measured their success and drew their blueprints based on another person's yardstick. But I believe that you should always have a goal that scares you. The purpose of a goal is to encourage us to grow and expand, and our goals should be worthy of our life. I think sometimes we get that mixed up. People limit their goals because they believe their goals should line up with who they are. What they don't realize is that who they are is a miracle. *You* are a miracle. Your goals need to be worthy of the miracle that you are. You need to have a goal that encourages you to expand, develop, and move forward infinitely.

Our goals are so important to us as entrepreneurs because we often rely on our own motivation to keep moving forward. We don't have someone above us giving us deadlines. We create our to-do lists. Our goals, from the small day-to-day tasks to our larger mission, all come from us. When you look at the vision and mission for your company, you have to ask yourself why does it exist? Who is your company servicing? What goals will help you achieve the larger mission that made you an entrepreneur in the first place?

As I've asked myself these questions, I've been able to use the answers to structure my goals and define my brand. During this process, a brand engineer reminded me that my vision has to be infinite. It *cannot* have an end.

If you have a vision and a mission for your company that's not infinite, you're going to reach it. And then what? You just close the company down, because you've achieved your vision and your mission?

You have to expand your goals so you can expand as a person, entrepreneur, and business leader. There is always room to expand. We limit ourselves when we name the one result that we want to reach. For some people, that result is making six figures. For others, that result is seven. For some, the goal is to help 1,000 people. For others, the goal is 1,000,000. All of these results can be achieved—and then what?

The answer isn't that you'll have the life that you want. We know that we're never satisfied when we achieve these limiting goals. Our journey, in business and in life, isn't about the destination—it's about the journey. We have one life to take a journey and enjoy an infinite number of opportunities. And we get to choose whether we love it or not. If you're not loving it, are you doing what you want with your life?

Embrace Infinite Temporary Defeats

Why aren't we enjoying the journey? Why are we so focused on the yardsticks of society? We're scared of failure. We're scared we aren't going to "measure up" or that we'll fall short of the blueprint we're drawing for ourselves. But the reality is there are always going to be "failures."

I don't typically use the word failure. I've taken a page from Napoleon Hill's *Think and Grow Rich*. Hill talks about the difference between *temporary defeat* versus failure. As an entrepreneur, I experience temporary defeats daily. In life, I've experienced temporary defeats. But I've always persevered.

Successful people persevere; they keep going in the face of the temporary defeat. And fortunately, when you have set infinite goals and chosen a journey that fuels your passion, you will naturally persevere past any temporary defeats. When you set goals that are worthy of your life, that bring their own momentum and pull you forward, it's not so hard to get out of bed in the morning.

This past year has taught everyone a lesson or two about temporary defeats. I delayed the launch of Amber Howard and Associates for months because of the COVID-19 pandemic. But in the process, I learned something important about temporary defeats. I reaffirmed the importance of being personally responsible for my own life—this is a key piece of the blueprint I have drawn for myself and my business. We always have a say in who we're going to be and how we're going to approach the circumstances of our life. We have an infinite number of choices to make that no one can ever take away from us. Until we take responsibility for those choices, recognize the power of infinity, and embrace the infinite amount of energy available to us throughout this journey, we are merely limiting ourselves.

Any time you want to create something new in your life, you have to kind of break through the limits and barriers that fear and terror create. Our brains do an excellent job at creating this fear. Part of what we do at Amber Howard and Associates is coach our clients in mindset—we're all about tearing down the barriers of fear. Our clients ask us the question that so many entrepreneurs ask as they start a business, set new goals, or try to take their business to the next level: what if it doesn't work out?

Well, what if it does? What if you set an infinite goal and you soar farther than you would have ever imagined? What if your business, your family, and your life is better than you could ever imagine?

This is the mindset that I'm all about at my business. Getting my clients into this mindset has been the ultimate goal. The resources, the people, the mentors, and the *how* of your journey will show up when you're ready for that. Everything will fall into place if you aim for infinity.

ALINKA'S FINAL THOUGHTS

B y the time you have finished this anthology, the world may have changed, your team may have handed you erasers, or your ideas may have aided you in seeing a new way to expand, grow, and build your business. That's just the nature of planning and creating a blueprint.

As we collect our pencils, erasers, whiteboards, blank sheets of paper, or whatever you use to plan out your six-figure blueprint, let's revisit some of the themes that our authors discussed throughout this anthology:

Perfecting your product or service

Think of Ben Hall, who practiced his banana pudding until it was perfect; or Anant Kataria, who ensured his customers that they would have the best service possible even through the pandemic. There *is* something to be said for creating the best offer that money can buy. Perfecting your craft, whether that is the products that you sell or the way that you show up for your team each and every day, directly impacts your blueprint and the possibilities for your business. What can you do to perfect your craft today?

Following your passion vs. following the money

The road from drawing a blueprint to seeing that blueprint being built is long and lonely. Entrepreneurship is tough. You need to work 16-hour days, seven-day weeks, and sacrifice vacations, events, and maybe even relationships. As our authors know, the sacrifices aren't going to be worth the reward if you absolutely hate your job. Six-figure blueprints offers a framework and a standard for choosing our authors, but don't follow the money. Passion and reinvention were the center of Max Ryerson's chapter. Following her passion brought Jody Steinhauer to a more profitable career than anything her parents could have wanted for her. Follow your passion. Where do you feel your drive taking you? What gets you excited to get up in the morning? Follow that, work hard, and the money will come.

Building a team to see your plans through

One of the toughest decisions an entrepreneur will face is when to hand over control to their team or employees. But think about a blueprint. The architect draws up the blueprint and gives it over to the team of construction workers. They make sure that plumbers, bricklayers, roofers, and a whole team of specialists are using their skills to properly build what is on their blueprint. The architect might put on a hard hat to assess the progress of the build, but if they expected to hammer each nail and frame each room on their own, the structure would never get built.

As Cindy Praeger wrote, "One person running a company can't scale."

Measuring, taking, and assessing risks

We all know that most startups do not last for more than a few years. As an entrepreneur, you've probably heard that from naysaying friends and realist partners. The moment you decide to draw up a blueprint, you are taking a risk. Each decision that you make comes with some level of risk. But as we learned from Brett Husak, calculating risks is always followed by seizing opportunities. Your ability to measure and assess risks will improve as your blueprints become more elaborate (or you are forced to erase lines or start anew). Pay attention to the risks that you take, but don't be afraid to *continue* the practice of taking them. Worst-case scenario, you walk away having learned something new.

As we move forward into the 2020s, I believe that many people will begin to live, plan, and build more comfortably with the knowledge that the world can change in an instant. Every day, however chaotic, tragic, or unstable, is an opportunity to draw up a new blueprint, change your floorplan, or continue building. With the knowledge, confidence, and advice that I hope you have gained from this anthology, your foundation will be more solid than ever.

So. . .

What's your plan?

ABOUT THE AUTHOR

Alinka Rutkowska is the CEO of Leaders Press (www.leaderspress.com), a USA Today and Wall Street Journal best-selling press, where she creates books for entrepreneurs from scratch and launches them to best-seller with a 100% success rate.

She runs a hybrid publishing house with traditional distribution (via Simon & Schuster) through which more than 500 entrepreneurs have been able to share their stories with the world.

172 of Leaders Press authors have become USA Today and Wall Street Journal best-selling authors.

Alinka has been featured by Forbes, Entrepreneur Magazine, Entrepreneurs on Fire and numerous other outlets.

Her mission is to help 10,000 entrepreneurs share their wisdom with the world by 2030.